JAVA API
FOR
DUMMIES®

Quick Reference

by Stephen D. Lockwood
and Madhu Siddalingaiah

™

IDG
BOOKS
WORLDWIDE

IDG Books Worldwide, Inc.
An International Data Group Company

Foster City, CA ✦ Chicago, IL ✦ Indianapolis, IN ✦ Southlake, TX

Java™ API For Dummies® Quick Reference

Published by
IDG Books Worldwide, Inc.
An International Data Group Company
919 E. Hillsdale Blvd.
Suite 400
Foster City, CA 94404
http://www.idgbooks.com (IDG Books Worldwide Web site)
http://www.dummies.com (Dummies Press Web site)

Library of Congress Catalog Card No.: 97-70749

ISBN: 0-7645-0118-6

Printed in the United States of America

10 9 8 7 6 5 4 3 2 1

1P/RV/QU/ZX/IN

Distributed in the United States by IDG Books Worldwide, Inc.

Distributed by Macmillan Canada for Canada; by Transworld Publishers Limited in the United Kingdom and Europe; by WoodsLane Pty. Ltd. for Australia; by WoodsLane Enterprises Ltd. for New Zealand; by Longman Singapore Publishers Ltd. for Singapore, Malaysia, Thailand, and Indonesia; by Simron Pty. Ltd. for South Africa; by Toppan Company Ltd. for Japan; by Distribuidora Cuspide for Argentina; by Livraria Cultura for Brazil; by Ediciencia S.A. for Ecuador; by Addison-Wesley Publishing Company for Korea; by Ediciones ZETA S.C.R. Ltda. for Peru; by WS Computer Publishing Company, Inc., for the Philippines; by Unalis Corporation for Taiwan; by Contemporanea de Ediciones for Venezuela. Authorized Sales Agent: Anthony Rudkin Associates for the Middle East and North Africa.

For general information on IDG Books Worldwide's books in the U.S., please call our Consumer Customer Service department at 800-762-2974. For reseller information, including discounts and premium sales, please call our Reseller Customer Service department at 800-434-3422.

For information on where to purchase IDG Books Worldwide's books outside the U.S., please contact our International Sales department at 415-655-3023 or fax 415-655-3299.

For information on foreign language translations, please contact our Foreign & Subsidiary Rights department at 415-655-3021 or fax 415-655-3281.

For sales inquiries and special prices for bulk quantities, please contact our Sales department at 415-655-3200 or write to the address above.

For information on using IDG Books Worldwide's books in the classroom or for ordering examination copies, please contact our Educational Sales department at 800-434-2086 or fax 817-251-8174.

For press review copies, author interviews, or other publicity information, please contact our Public Relations department at 415-655-3000 or fax 415-655-3299.

For authorization to photocopy items for corporate, personal, or educational use, please contact Copyright Clearance Center, 222 Rosewood Drive, Danvers, MA 01923, or fax 508-750-4470.

is a trademark under exclusive
license to IDG Books Worldwide, Inc.,
from International Data Group, Inc.

About the Authors

Steve Lockwood: Steve is one of the founders of PraxisNET, a Washington, D.C., based Java development firm. Steve teaches Java and Web related courses for large corporations and government agencies through Learning Tree International. Steve is also the coauthor of *Java How-To,* published by Waite Group Press.

Steve received his B.S. (magna cum laude) in Engineering Physics from Embry Riddle Aeronautical University in Daytona Beach. He specializes in helping people understand and exploit emerging technologies — such as Java. He lives along the Chesapeake Bay with his wife Valerie and can be found on their Sea-Doo whenever the weather is nice.

Madhu Siddalingaiah: Madhu is one of the founders of PraxisNET, a Washington, D.C., based Java development firm. Madhu teaches Java and Web related courses for large corporations and government agencies through Learning Tree International. Madhu is also the coauthor of *Java How-To,* published by Waite Group Press.

Madhu received his B.S. in Physics from the University of Maryland. Madhu was first exposed to the Arpanet (Internet) in 1983; since then he has maintained interest in emerging technologies, such as the World Wide Web and Java. Madhu has worked with world leaders in the areas of hardware design, digital signal processing, research satellite instrumentation, 3D graphics, and communications receivers. In his spare time, Madhu can be found flying helicopters and attempting to play guitar — but not at the same time.

ABOUT IDG BOOKS WORLDWIDE

Welcome to the world of IDG Books Worldwide.

IDG Books Worldwide, Inc., is a subsidiary of International Data Group, the world's largest publisher of computer-related information and the leading global provider of information services on information technology. IDG was founded more than 25 years ago and now employs more than 8,500 people worldwide. IDG publishes more than 275 computer publications in over 75 countries (see listing below). More than 60 million people read one or more IDG publications each month.

Launched in 1990, IDG Books Worldwide is today the #1 publisher of best-selling computer books in the United States. We are proud to have received eight awards from the Computer Press Association in recognition of editorial excellence and three from *Computer Currents'* First Annual Readers' Choice Awards. Our best-selling *...For Dummies®* series has more than 30 million copies in print with translations in 30 languages. IDG Books Worldwide, through a joint venture with IDG's Hi-Tech Beijing, became the first U.S. publisher to publish a computer book in the People's Republic of China. In record time, IDG Books Worldwide has become the first choice for millions of readers around the world who want to learn how to better manage their businesses.

Our mission is simple: Every one of our books is designed to bring extra value and skill-building instructions to the reader. Our books are written by experts who understand and care about our readers. The knowledge base of our editorial staff comes from years of experience in publishing, education, and journalism — experience we use to produce books for the '90s. In short, we care about books, so we attract the best people. We devote special attention to details such as audience, interior design, use of icons, and illustrations. And because we use an efficient process of authoring, editing, and desktop publishing our books electronically, we can spend more time ensuring superior content and spend less time on the technicalities of making books.

You can count on our commitment to deliver high-quality books at competitive prices on topics you want to read about. At IDG Books Worldwide, we continue in the IDG tradition of delivering quality for more than 25 years. You'll find no better book on a subject than one from IDG Books Worldwide.

John Kilcullen

John Kilcullen
CEO
IDG Books Worldwide, Inc.

WINNER	WINNER		WINNER	WINNER
Eighth Annual Computer Press Awards ≥1992	*Ninth Annual Computer Press Awards ≥1993*		*Tenth Annual Computer Press Awards ≥1994*	*Eleventh Annual Computer Press Awards ≥1995*

IDG Books Worldwide, Inc., is a subsidiary of International Data Group, the world's largest publisher of computer-related information and the leading global provider of information services on information technology. International Data Group publishes over 275 computer publications in over 75 countries. Sixty million people read one or more International Data Group publications each month. International Data Group's publications include: ARGENTINA: Buyer's Guide, Computerworld Argentina, PC World Argentina; AUSTRALIA: Australian Macworld, Australian PC World, Australian Reseller News, Computerworld, IT Casebook, Network World, Publish, Webmaster; AUSTRIA: Computerwelt Osterreich, Networks Austria, PC Tip Austria; BANGLADESH: PC World Bangladesh; BELARUS: PC World Belarus; BELGIUM: Data News; BRAZIL: Annuário de Informática, Computerworld, Connections, Macworld, PC Player, PC World, Publish, Reseller News, Supergamepower; BULGARIA: Computerworld Bulgaria, Network World Bulgaria, PC & MacWorld Bulgaria; CANADA: CIO Canada, Client/Server World, ComputerWorld Canada, InfoWorld Canada, NetworkWorld Canada, WebWorld; CHILE: Computerworld Chile, PC World Chile; COLOMBIA: Computerworld Colombia, PC World Colombia; COSTA RICA: PC World Centro America; THE CZECH AND SLOVAK REPUBLICS: Computerworld Czechoslovakia, Macworld Czech Republic, PC World Czechoslovakia; DENMARK: Communications World Danmark, Computerworld Danmark, Macworld Danmark, PC World Danmark, Techworld Denmark; DOMINICAN REPUBLIC: PC World Republica Dominicana; ECUADOR: PC World Ecuador; EGYPT: Computerworld Middle East, PC World Middle East; EL SALVADOR: PC World Centro America; FINLAND: MikroPC, Tietoverkko, Tietoviikko; FRANCE: Distributique, Hebdo, Info PC, Le Monde Informatique, Macworld, Reseaux & Telecoms, WebMaster France; GERMANY: Computer Partner, Computerwoche, Computerwoche Extra, Computerwoche FOCUS, Global Online, Macwelt, PC Welt; GREECE: Amiga Computing, GamePro Greece, Multimedia World; GUATEMALA: PC World Centro America; HONDURAS: PC World Centro America; HONG KONG: Computerworld Hong Kong, PC World Hong Kong, Publish in Asia; HUNGARY: ABCD CD-ROM, Computerworld Szamitastechnika, Internetto online Magazine, PC World Hungary, PC-X Magazin Hungary; ICELAND: Tolvuheimur PC World Island; INDIA: Information Communications World, Information Systems Computerworld, PC World India, Publish in Asia; INDONESIA: InfoKomputer PC World, Komputek Computerworld, Publish in Asia; IRELAND: ComputerScope, PC Live!; ISRAEL: Macworld Israel, People & Computers/Computerworld; ITALY: Computerworld Italia, Macworld Italia, Networking Italia, PC World Italia; JAPAN: DTP World, Macworld Japan, Nikkei Personal Computing, OS/2 World Japan, SunWorld Japan, Windows NT World, Windows World Japan; KENYA: PC World East African; KOREA: Hi-Tech Information, Macworld Korea, PC World Korea, MACEDONIA: PC World Macedonia; MALAYSIA: Computerworld Malaysia, PC World Malaysia, Publish in Asia; MALTA: PC World Malta; MEXICO: Computerworld Mexico, PC World Mexico; MYANMAR: PC World Myanmar; NETHERLANDS: Computer! Totaal, LAN Internetworking Magazine, LAN World Buyers Guide, Macworld Netherlands, Net, WebWorld; NEW ZEALAND: Absolute Beginners Guide and Plain & Simple Series, Computer Buyer, Computer Industry Directory, Computerworld New Zealand, MTB, Network World, PC World New Zealand; NICARAGUA: PC World Centro America; NORWAY: Computerworld Norge, CW Rapport, Datamagasinet, Financial Rapport, Kursguide Norge, Macworld Norge, Multimediaworld Norge, PC World Ekspress Norge, PC World Nettverk, PC World Norge, PC World ProduktGuide Norge; PAKISTAN: Computerworld Pakistan; PANAMA: PC World Panama; PEOPLE'S REPUBLIC OF CHINA: China Computer Users, China Computerworld, China InfoWorld, China Telecom World Weekly, Computer & Communication, Electronic Design China, Electronics Today, Electronics Weekly, Game Software, PC World China, Popular Computer Week, Software Weekly, Software World, Telecom World; PERU: Computerworld Peru, PC World Profesional Peru, PC World SoHo Peru; PHILIPPINES: Click!, Computerworld Philippines, PC World Philippines, Publish in Asia; POLAND: Computerworld Poland, Computerworld Special Report Poland, Cyber, Macworld Poland, Networld Poland, PC World Komputer; PORTUGAL: Cerebro/PC World, Computerworld/Correio Informático, Dealer World Portugal, Mac*In/PC*In Portugal, Multimedia World; PUERTO RICO: PC World Puerto Rico; ROMANIA: Computerworld Romania, PC World Romania, Telecom Romania; RUSSIA: Computerworld Russia, Mir PK, Publish, Seti; SINGAPORE: Computerworld Singapore, PC World Singapore, Publish in Asia; SLOVENIA: Monitor; SOUTH AFRICA: Computing SA, Network World SA, Software World SA; SPAIN: Communicaciones World Espana, Computerworld Espana, Computerworld Espana, PC World Espana; SRI LANKA: Infolink PC World; SWEDEN: CAP&Design, Computer Sweden, Corporate Computing Sweden, Internetworld Sweden, it.branschen, Macworld Sweden, MaxiData Sweden, MikroDatorn, Natverk & Kommunikation, PC World Sweden, PCaktiv, Windows World Sweden; SWITZERLAND: Computerworld Schweiz, Macworld Schweiz, PCtip; TAIWAN: Computerworld Taiwan, Macworld Taiwan, NEW ViSiON/Publish, PC World Taiwan, Windows World Taiwan; THAILAND: Publish in Asia, Thai Computerworld; TURKEY: Computerworld Turkiye, Macworld Turkiye, Network World Turkiye, PC World Turkiye; UKRAINE: Computerworld Kiev, Multimedia World Ukraine, PC World Ukraine; UNITED KINGDOM: Acorn User UK, Amiga Action UK, Amiga Computing UK, Apple Talk UK, Computing, Macworld, Parents and Computers UK, PC Advisor, PC Home, PSX Pro, The WEB; UNITED STATES: Cable in the Classroom, CIO Magazine, Computerworld, DOS World, Federal Computer Week, GamePro Magazine, InfoWorld, I-Way, Macworld, Network World, PC Games, PC World, Publish, Video Event, THE WEB Magazine, and WebMaster; online webzines: JavaWorld, NetscapeWorld, and SunWorld Online; URUGUAY: InfoWorld Uruguay; VENEZUELA: Computerworld Venezuela, PC World Venezuela; and VIETNAM: PC World Vietnam. 2/14/97

Dedication

Steve: To Dad, for your support which allowed me to gain the knowledge required to make this book possible.

Madhu: To my parents, Vimala and Honnappa.

Authors' Acknowledgments

A number of people contributed to this book and deserve our thanks. First, we would like to thank Jill Pisoni and Mary Goodwin at IDG Books Worldwide, Inc., for being so patient and helpful throughout the writing process. In addition, we would like to thank Vartan Piroumian for producing the class hierarchy diagrams that appear throughout the book. Tracy Logsdon and Larry Bohning helped check the technical content and accuracy.

Special thanks to Roy DeMott for all his creative help and artistic talent, and to Dr. J. Michael Picone for his enlightened consultation. Also, we would like to thank R. Jack Chapman and Praxis, Inc., for supplying facilities and resources without which this book would not have been possible.

Publisher's Acknowledgments

We're proud of this book; please send us your comments about it by using the IDG Books Worldwide Registration Card at the back of the book or by e-mailing us at feedback/dummies@idgbooks.com. Some of the people who helped bring this book to market include the following:

Acquisitions, Development, and Editorial

Project Editor: Mary Goodwin

Senior Acquisitions Editor: Jill Pisoni

Product Development Director: Mary Bednarek

Copy Editor: Michael Simsic

Technical Editor: Vartan Piroumian

Editorial Manager: Mary C. Corder

Editorial Assistants: Chris H. Collins, Steven H. Hayes, Michael D. Sullivan

Production

Associate Project Coordinator: E. Shawn Aylsworth

Layout and Graphics: Brett Black, Cameron Booker, Dominique DeFelice, Angela F. Hunckler, Todd Klemme, Drew R. Moore, Mark Owens, Brent Savage

Special Art: Roy DeMott

Proofreaders: Laura L. Bowman, Arielle Carole Mennelle, Joel K. Draper, Nancy Price, Dwight Ramsey

---

General and Administrative

IDG Books Worldwide, Inc.: John Kilcullen, CEO; Steven Berkowitz, President and Publisher

IDG Books Technology Publishing: Brenda McLaughlin, Senior Vice President and Group Publisher

Dummies Technology Press and Dummies Editorial: Diane Graves Steele, Vice President and Associate Publisher; Judith A. Taylor, Brand Manager; Kristin A. Cocks, Editorial Director

Dummies Trade Press: Kathleen A. Welton, Vice President and Publisher; Stacy S. Collins, Brand Manager

IDG Books Production for Dummies Press: Beth Jenkins, Production Director; Cindy L. Phipps, Supervisor of Project Coordination, Production Proofreading, and Indexing; Kathie S. Schutte, Supervisor of Page Layout; Shelley Lea, Supervisor of Graphics and Design; Debbie J. Gates, Production Systems Specialist; Tony Augsburger, Supervisor of Reprints and Bluelines; Leslie Popplewell, Media Archive Coordinator

Dummies Packaging and Book Design: Patti Sandez, Packaging Specialist; Lance Kayser, Packaging Assistant; Kavish + Kavish, Cover Design

✦

The publisher would like to give special thanks to Patrick J. McGovern, without whom this book would not have been possible.

✦

Table of Contents

How to Use This Book

Welcome to *Java API For Dummies Quick Reference*, an easy-to-use reference for both advanced and beginner Java programmers. Regardless of how much you have worked with Java, at some time you may have questions or need a refresher about the Java API, Java syntax, or applet security. You can keep *Java API For Dummies Quick Reference* right beside your computer (yes, it's small enough, it will fit) and reach for the book any time you have a question or need some help.

Java API For Dummies Quick Reference differs from most of the computer books you see on the shelf. Those other books walk you through programming from square one, but they don't help you if you just want a quick answer to a question you have. Rather than fumbling through pages and pages of text that you really don't need or want to read, you can pick up *Java API For Dummies Quick Reference* and find out just what you want to know.

Who You Are

One thing you need to know about this book from the get-go is that it does not teach you about Java and Java programming from the ground up. You should use this book when you're in the middle of writing a program or applet and you forget how to do a particular thing, or you forget what a certain term means. Think of this book as a fast-and-furious, in-and-out reference rather than a hand-held, guided tour of the basics of Java and the common packages of the API.

If you feel you may need more help getting started with Java and Java programming, we heartily recommend that you pick up a copy of *Java For Dummies,* by Aaron E. Walsh, also published by IDG Books Worldwide, Inc. Aaron's book takes an in-depth look at the language starting from ground zero. Another book that may be of help is *Java Programming For Dummies,* by Donald J. Koosis and David Koosis, also published by IDG Books Worldwide. Donald and David's book explains the ins and outs of Java programming.

Why You Want to Learn Java

Java is by far the fastest growing language to date. It is simple, powerful, and ubiquitous. Using Java, you can build dazzling Web pages with real time interaction, networked front ends for data display, and sophisticated cross-platform applications. Certainly, you could use other Web technologies and other languages to construct your pages, but if you want true platform independence, Java can't be beat. Is Java the final word in computing? Probably not, but Java has already made its mark in history and will probably change the way we use computers.

What You Need to Get Started

One of the many smart things that Sun Microsystems, the creators of Java, did to promote Java was to make the Java developers kit (JDK) freely available on their Web site (http://www.javasoft. com). On the Web site, you can get free JDKs for almost all major platforms. In addition, many vendors offer developed integrated development tools which can improve programmer productivity.

To get started, download the JDK for your platform or purchase one of the commercial development tools and then jump in. You may also want to get one of the Java enabled browsers, such as Netscape Navigator or Microsoft Internet Explorer, to help you view your applications.

How This Book Is Organized

Many of you may have questions about the language syntax and the development tools used to write Java programs. The first couple of parts of this book are for you — they focus on the language syntax. The other parts of this book discuss the building blocks of the language — the libraries of Java classes that you use when writing a Java program.

Part I: Getting to Know Java

Part I presents some essential information about Java-related HTML syntax. In addition, we tell you what you need to know about applet security. These concepts are vital to writing Java programs and using applets in your Web page.

Part II: The Java Language Syntax

Part II features the syntax of Java, covering topics such as re-served keywords, primitive data types, and modifiers. This is the part of the book where you hear all about the rules that govern the Java language.

You may find this part of the book very helpful — it's not easy to remember all permutations of class, interface, and method modifiers. You can also easily forget the precedence of some of the operators. In either case, the syntax section offers easy-to-refer-to tables that will come in handy when you need a quick answer.

Part III: The Java Core API

Most of the time, you have a good idea of what you want to do with an application, but you can't remember the name of a method you need. Or maybe you can't remember a class that you don't use often enough to memorize. Part III, the largest part of the book, can refresh your memory when a particular method or class escapes you.

In this part, you find the Java core API listed in alphabetical order by package. We cover the following packages: applet, awt, awt.datatransfer, awt.event, awt.image, io, lang, net, sql, util, and util.zip. We also diagram each package to show the relationship of all classes in that package. Following each diagram we list all the classes and contained methods, variables, and fields for the package along with a summary and explanation of each. We hope the hierarchy diagrams and their accompanying explanations give you a picture that can help make sense of it all.

Part IV: Java Errors and Exceptions

Consider this part your Java safety net. You can come here when you get that uncomfortable feeling that something may have gone wrong. In the part, you find hierarchy diagrams of all errors and exceptions you may run across when working with Java packages discussed in this book. We use hierarchy diagrams to help you sort out all the errors and exceptions you can face when working with Java.

Ways to Use This Book

You have a number of ways to use this book. You can look at the Table of Contents to identify topics that are of interest to you, or you can simply flip through the various parts and preview the information they contain. Perhaps the best way to use this book is to keep it handy as you program and turn to the index to locate the material that you need. The index can be used to quickly locate all information in the book; you find all the packages and their corresponding classes and contained methods, variables, and fields listed in the index.

We list all the packages in Part III in alphabetical order so that you can find them quickly. Within each package, the classes and their methods are also listed alphabetically.

Conventions Used in This Book

As you read this book, you'll notice that some text — method names, class names, and HTML code, for example — appears in a different font than the rest of the text. We use the different font to make those items easy for you to spot in the text. When we discuss HTML syntax in Part I, required elements appear in **bold,** optional elements appear in regular typeface, and elements you specify appear in *italics*. In Parts III and IV, we use bold to distinguish the various methods and fields within a class. All of these conventions help make it even easier for you to find the information you need.

What the Little Pictures Mean

You see little pictures, called *icons,* sprinkled generously throughout this book. These icons help you locate — in an instant — some key points about a topic. Here's what the icons in this book mean:

This icon flags parts of the book that help you do something neat or save you time and money.

Never ignore this icon, even if you ignore all the other icons. This icon flags areas where you need to be careful to avoid some unpleasant result.

 This icon points out real-life examples of the subject at hand.

 C or C++ programmers should be on the lookout for concepts that may be slightly different in Java than they are in C or C++. If you're not a C programmer, you can skip these icons.

 This icon sends you to an appropriate point in *Java Programming For Dummies* or *Java For Dummies* for more information about a task.

What's Next?

It's time to start brewing some Java, that's what! The best way to learn Java (or any programming language, for that matter) is to just jump in and write code, lots of code. No tool, trick, or magic wand can replace the knowledge you gain from experience.

The best programmers may not be geniuses by any objective measure, but no one can dispute that a good programmer brings an artistry to the task. Good programmers try to create code with a sense of symmetry, simplicity, and flow. In fact, the programmers who created Java used some of these subjective standards to define the language.

Michelangelo once looked at a huge hunk of unfinished rock and said that the sculpture was already there — he only needed to remove the unnecessary marble to uncover it. The same could be said of programming. The next time you're sitting in front of an empty source file, picture the code and then mentally knock away the bits you don't need.

Part 1

Getting to Know Java

Java is a fully functional object-oriented programming language that allows you to develop applications and applets. You can develop stand-alone applications in Java as you can in other languages. You also can create Java applets to embed into World Wide Web (Web) pages. These applets are dynamically downloaded to the client machine along with the Web page and are executed locally inside the browser.

Java is a platform-independent language. All major platforms currently have Java interpreters, and additional interpreters are in development.

In this part, you get some basic information about working with Java. We give you the low-down on what you need to know about Java-related HTML syntax and applet security.

In this part . . .

✔ Using Java-related HTML syntax

✔ Understanding applet security

Looking at Java-Related HTML Syntax

HTML is an evolving standard, and the APPLET tag is evolving with it. Applets, with all their capabilities, are what popularized Java, even though Java is much more than just simple animations on Web pages.

In this section, we show you the complete syntax for the APPLET tag (which you use to embed a Java applet in your Web page) with all its possible attributes — hurray, just what you always wanted, right? After we show you the complete syntax, we explain each of its elements. In the following sections, optional elements appear in regular typeface, and elements you specify appear in italics. Mandatory elements appear in bold.

As a reminder, *tags* are HTML elements that appear after a less-than (<) character. *Attributes* are other elements that reside inside the less-than and greater-than characters (<>). Some attributes are mandatory. You'll understand why they are mandatory when you see them.

Looking at the complete APPLET tag syntax

Without further ado, we present the complete syntax for the APPLET tag:

```
<APPLET
CODEBASE = codebaseURL
ARCHIVES = archivesList
CODE = appletFile ...or... OBJECT = serializedApplet
ALT = alternateText
NAME = appletInstanceName
WIDTH = pixels HEIGHT = pixels
ALIGN = alignment
VSPACE = pixels HSPACE = pixels
    >
<PARAM NAME = appletAttribute1 VALUE = value>
<PARAM NAME = appletAttribute2 VALUE = value>
. . .
alternateHTML
</APPLET>
```

CODEBASE, ARCHIVES, CODE, and the other elements inside the APPLET tag are attributes of the APPLET tag; they give the browser information about the APPLET tag. CODE, WIDTH, and HEIGHT are the only mandatory attributes and must always be specified. The details of the attributes are described in the following sections.

CODEBASE = codebaseURL

This optional attribute specifies the base URL of the applet — the directory on the server that contains the applet's code. If you don't specify the CODEBASE attribute, then the document's URL is used. You use CODEBASE = codebaseURL only when the applet does not reside in the same directory as the HTML file.

ARCHIVES = archivesList

ARCHIVES = archivesList is an optional attribute that describes one or more archives containing classes and other resources (images and sound, for example) that will be "preloaded." Archives provide a way of reducing download time.

Java loads the classes using an instance of an AppletClassLoader with the given CODEBASE. In JDK1.1, multiple APPLET tags with the same CODEBASE share the same instance of a ClassLoader. This shared instance can be used by client code to implement inter-applet communication. JDK1.2 may provide a cleaner mechanism for inter-applet communication and may give each APPLET instance its own ClassLoader instance, thus improving security.

CODE = appletFile

A required attribute, CODE = appletFile gives the name of the file that contains the applet's compiled applet subclass. This file is relative to the CODEBASE base URL of the applet. Either CODE or OBJECT must be present in the applet.

OBJECT = serializedApplet

This attribute gives the name of the file that contains a serialized representation of an applet. Either the CODE or OBJECT attribute must be specified. The applet will be deserialized when it is downloaded. The applet's init() method will *not* be invoked, but its start() method will. This differs from the CODE attribute, in which the applet's init() method is called before the start() method. Attributes valid when the original object was serialized are *not* restored.

Any attributes passed to this applet instance will be available to the applet; we advocate restraint in using this feature. An applet should be stopped before it is serialized.

ALT = alternateText

This optional attribute specifies any text that should be displayed if the browser understands the APPLET tag but can't run Java applets. It's like the ALT attribute in an IMG tag, with which you may be familiar if you have worked with HTML.

NAME = appletInstanceName

This optional attribute specifies a name for the applet instance, which makes it possible for applets on the same page to find (and communicate with) each other. You don't need to use this attribute unless you plan to communicate between applets.

WIDTH = pixels and HEIGHT = pixels

These required attributes determine the width and height (in pixels) of the applet display area, not counting any windows or dialog boxes that the applet may create.

ALIGN = alignment

This optional attribute specifies the alignment of the applet. The possible values of this attribute are the same as those for the IMG tag: left, right, top, texttop, middle, absmiddle, baseline, bottom, absbottom. You should experiment with these values to see which combination works best with your applets.

VSPACE = pixels and HSPACE = pixels

These optional attributes specify the number of pixels above and below the applet (VSPACE) and on each side of the applet (HSPACE). You treat these attributes the same way as you do the IMG tag's VSPACE and HSPACE attributes (see ALIGN = alignment in this part).

The Applet parameter tag

The following tag is the only way to specify an applet-specific parameter:

```
<PARAM NAME = appletAttribute1 VALUE = value>
<PARAM NAME = appletAttribute2 VALUE = value> . . .
```

Applets can retrieve their parameters with the getParameter() method. Remember that PARAM tags can appear only in between <APPLET> and </APPLET> tags. Also note that PARAM NAME attributes should be unique.

Don't use any of the applet attribute elements as parameter names, which may result in a conflict (some browsers get confused easily). For example, don't use parameters such as these:

```
<PARAM NAME = WIDTH VALUE = value>
<PARAM NAME = CODE VALUE = value> . . .
```

Placing an applet on a page

In this section, we show you an example that places an applet, called `PhoneBook`, on a Web page. The applet lists phone numbers which are stored in a file on the server. The width and height of this applet is 400 by 500 pixels, respectively. An applet parameter specifies the name of a file on the server containing the telephone numbers so that an HTML author can easily change the file name without bothering a Java programmer.

```
<APPLET CODE = "PhoneBook.class" WIDTH = "400" Height = "500">
<PARAM NAME = "index" VALUE = "personal.dat">
<CENTER><H1>NOTICE</H1></CENTER>
<B>This page contains a Java applet. Your browser is either not
    capable of executing Java applets or you have that option
    turned off. Please obtain a Java enabled browser or turn on
    execution of Java.</B>
</APPLET>
```

Java-enabled browsers ignore all other HTML tags that appear between the `<APPLET>` and `</APPLET>` tags. Non Java-enabled browsers ignore all the Java related tags (because they don't understand the tags) and display any available additional tags.

Understanding Applet Security

Some of Java's critics have called applets a laboratory for viruses. Think of some of the obvious hacks that could befall an unsuspecting Web surfer, such as retrieving password files, deleting files, filling your hard drive with useless data, or compromising a firewall. Fortunately, none of these operations (including other, more subtle hacks) are possible because *untrusted applets* (applets that are not digitally signed by a trusted source) are restricted by applet security. If applet security was not as tight as it is, Java would have died before it ever saw its first Web server.

An applet must overcome several hurdles before it can be executed on a remote machine. The class loader, the security manager, and the virtual machine itself are what allow good to triumph over evil, order over chaos, the very survival of humanity! Well, maybe not the future of humanity, but you get the picture.

The following list details operations that untrusted applets can't perform:

✦ Access the local file system, including reading, writing, deleting, renaming, or obtaining file information

✦ Execute native code on the local machine via `Runtime.exec()`

✦ Create a network connection to any computer other than the machine from which the applet was loaded

✦ Listen for or accept socket connections from any port

✦ Create a frame or dialog without a visible warning indicating the untrusted nature of the applet that created the frame or dialog

✦ Define system properties

✦ Invoke `System.exit ()`

✦ Load dynamic libraries using `load()` or `loadLibrary ()`

✦ Create or manipulate any thread that is not part of the same threadgroup as the applet itself

✦ Create a `ClassLoader` or `SecurityManager` object

✦ Define any of the "Factories," such as `ContentHandlerFactory`, `SockImplFactory`, or `URLStreamFactory`

Part II

The Java Language Syntax

Before you can speak any language, including English or Computerese, you must first understand the syntax of the language. Because syntax is as important with Java as it is with any language, we devote this entire part of the book to the topic. This part contains many tables and lists to which you can refer during your long nights of programming.

If you've programmed in C or C++, some sections in this part may seem familiar to you. That's because Java syntax is similar to C and C++. Java does differ from C and C++ in one important way: Java doesn't try to be backward compatible with C. You can compile C code with the C++ compiler, but you can't even get close to C code with the Java compiler.

However, most of the syntax in Java is similar to C. Variable declarations, expressions, and flow control constructs in Java are very similar to C and C++.

In this part . . .

- ✔ Casting
- ✔ Using character escape sequences
- ✔ Commenting about comments
- ✔ Modifying properties
- ✔ Operating in Java
- ✔ Understanding primitive data types
- ✔ Avoiding reserved keywords

Casting

Casting is the conversion of a variable from one type to another. Java does not allow casting between arbitrary types. However, Java does allow casting between numeric types and between subclasses and superclasses of the same objects. When casting from a smaller to a larger type (for example, from `byte` to `int`) or from a subclass to a superclass, you don't have to use an explicit cast.

When you do a lossy cast (for example, from `int` to `byte`), you need to use an explicit cast, and the conversion is done modulo the length of the smaller type. You also need to use an explicit cast when you want to cast from a superclass to a subclass. Illegal casts will throw a `ClassCastException` at runtime.

In Java, boolean is a distinct data type that can't be cast into any other type, and no other type may be cast into a boolean.

Character Escape Sequences

The primitive data type `char` is used for single characters. However, Java includes several "special" characters that represent codes and are difficult to type directly, including backspace and carriage return. You can use an escape sequence to represent these characters, which may be useful if you need to include one of these codes in a `String` or as a character.

To include a tab in a text `String`, use something like the following line:

```
String myString = "Part II. \t The Java Language Syntax";
```

The following table lists escape sequences with their corresponding character and Unicode values:

Escape Sequence	Unicode Value	Character Value
\b	\u0008	Backspace
\t	\u0009	Horizontal tab
\n	\u000a	Newline
\f	\u000c	Form feed
\r	\u000d	Carriage return
\"	\u0022	Double quote
\'	\u0027	Single quote
\\	\u005c	Backslash
\uxxxx	\u0000 to \u00ff	Unicode character

Commenting about Comments

Java supports the same comments available in C and C++ (/*, */, and //), as well as special *javadoc comments*. The compiler treats javadoc comments the same as any other comment; however, these comments can also be extracted with the javadoc tool. The javadoc tool automatically parses class, interface, method, and variable declarations and produces reference documentation in HTML format from the javadoc comments placed in your code.

The javadoc tool is an extremely useful tool that creates consistent and professional-looking documentation for all your code. Because the comments are embedded in the actual source code, you can ensure that all your documentation is always up to date. Whenever the source code is modified, simply run javadoc again to produce a new set of documentation.

Constructing javadoc comments

You can place javadoc comments in your code by starting the comment with /** and ending the comment with */. You place javadoc comments immediately before a class, method, or variable declaration to allow you to supply documentation with a description.

The first sentence of each javadoc comment should be a summary sentence containing a concise but complete description of the item being discussed. This initial summary sentence ends at the first period, which is followed by a blank, tab, line terminator, or first javadoc tag.

The javadoc tool produces the documentation as HTML format files that can be viewed in any Web browser. You may include HTML tags in your javadoc comments, but you should not include HTML structural tags such as <H1> or <HR>. Because the documentation is in HTML format, you can add HTML tags to your comments that allow you to format the documentation.

Using javadoc tags

javadoc parses special tags, which begin with the at-sign character (@). javadoc recognizes these special tags when they are embedded within a javadoc comment; the tags allow additional formatting for the documentation. You can also use them to add information, such as the author name and version number.

If you want your javadoc comment to contain such tags, you must place the tags on the first line of the comment. If you use more than one tag with the same name, you should put the tags together on subsequent lines so that javadoc can tell where the list ends.

The following table lists the available tags for `javadoc`:

Tag	Function
`@see classname` and `@see classname(#)method-name`	Adds a hyperlinked See Also entry to the class. You also can use the hashmark character (#) to separate the name of a class from the name of one of its fields, methods, or constructors. You can select an overloaded method or constructor by including a parenthesized list of argument types after the method or constructor name. A javadoc comment may contain more than one @see tag, which can appear before class, method, and variable definitions.
`@version version-text`	Adds a Version: entry to the documentation. A javadoc comment can contain only one @version tag, which can appear only before a class definition. Make use of any version entry you like to help you identify or describe the code.
`@author name-text`	Adds an Author: entry to the documentation. A javadoc comment may contain multiple @author tags, which can appear only before a class definition. The author entry usually contains the code.
`@param parameter-name description`	Adds the specified parameter and description to the Parameters: section of the documentation. You can describe all input parameters to the method. This tag can be used only before a method definition. If you're feeling verbose, you can continue the description on the next line.
`@return description`	Adds a Returns: section, which contains the specified description of the return value. This tag describes the value of the method, and you can use it only before a method definition.
`@exception fully-qualified-class-name description`	Adds a Throws: entry, which contains the name of the exception that may be thrown by the method. The exception is automatically linked to its class documentation. You can use this tag only before a method definition.

We show you a few examples of @see comments in the following list:

```
@see java.lang.String
@see String#equals
@see java.lang.Object#wait(int)
@see <a href="spec.html">Java Spec</a>
```

Just in case you always wanted to see an example of a javadoc comment, take a look at this comment you could place before a class definition:

```
/**
 * A class representing an improved Date.
 * For example:
 * <pre>
 *          MyDate today = new MyDate();
 * </pre>
 *
 * @see                     util.Date
 * @version         2.1 Feb 26, 1997
 * @author          Steve Lockwood
 * @author          Madhu Siddalingaiah
 */
class MyDate extends Date {
// Body of class not shown
}
```

To see an example of a comment that you can place before a method definition, sneak a peek at the following:

```
/**
 * Converts a String value to a double
 * For example:
 * <pre>
 *          double dvalue = stringToDouble(strvalue);
 * </pre>
 *
 * @param          strvalue the String to convert
 * @return the converted double value
 */
public double stringToDouble (String strvalue) {
          // Method body not shown
}
```

The following figure shows the HTML page that you could generate using javadoc from the preceding two javadoc comment examples:

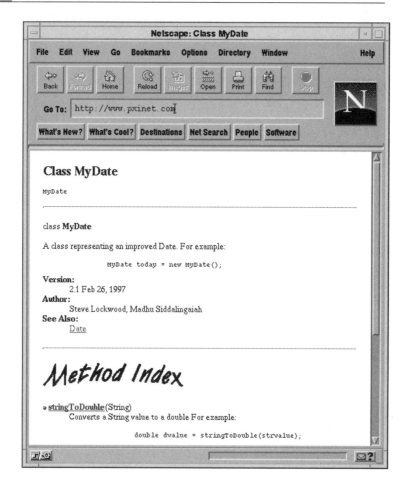

Modifying Properties

Modifiers, believe it or not, modify the properties of classes, interfaces, methods, and variables. Modifiers can be sorted into two categories: visibility modifiers and attribute modifiers. The *visibility modifiers* control the accessibility, or *visibility*, of classes, interfaces, methods, and variables from other classes and methods. Basically, visibility modifiers control which classes and methods can see which classes and methods. For example, if a class is declared public, the class can be used by any other class.

The following table lists the visibility modifiers available in Java:

Modifier	Acts On	Description
public	class	Visible anywhere
	interface	Visible anywhere
	method	Visible anywhere its class is visible
	variable	Visible anywhere its class is visible
protected	class	N/A
	interface	N/A
	method	Visible throughout the package and in any subclass
	variable	Visible throughout the package and in any subclass
no modifier (default)	class	Visible within package
	interface	Visible within package
	method	Visible within package
	variable	Visible within package
private	class	N/A
	interface	N/A
	method	Visible within its own class
	variable	Visible within its own class

Java offers other modifiers, called *attribute modifiers,* which specify a number of attributes of classes, interfaces, methods, and variables.

The following table lists the attribute modifiers in Java for your enjoyment:

Modifier	Acts On	Description
abstract	class	Contains abstract methods and can't be instantiated directly.
	interface	All interfaces are abstract, and the modifier is optional.
	method	No body is provided for the method, and the signature is followed by a semicolon. Class must also be abstract.
	variable	N/A
final	class	Can't be subclassed.
	interface	N/A
	method	Can't be overridden.
	variable	Value can't be changed (behaves like a constant).
native	class	N/A
	interface	N/A
	method	Implemented in a non-Java language (C or C++, for example). No body is provided, and the signature is followed by a semicolon.
	variable	N/A

(continued)

Modifier	Acts On	Description
static	class	N/A
	interface	N/A
	method	Method is a *class method,* meaning that it can't refer to non-static variables or methods of the class. Method is implicitly final and must be invoked through the class name.
	variable	Variable is a *class variable*, meaning that there is only one instance, no matter how many class instances are created. It must be accessed through the class name.
synchronized	class	N/A
	interface	N/A
	method	A lock for the class is acquired before execution, which ensures only one synchronized method can be running per class.
	variable	N/A

Dealing with Operators

The Java language contains various operators that perform many functions — from mathematical addition to a boolean logical expression.

The following table lists the Java operators in order of highest precedence to lowest (the *precedence* is the order in which the operators will be evaluated):

Precedence	Operator	Type (s)	Operation Performed
1	++	Arithmetic	Pre or post increment
	−	Arithmetic	Pre or post decrement
	+, -	Arithmetic	Unary plus and unary minus
	~	Integral	Bitwise complement
	!	Boolean	Logical complement
	(type)	Any	Cast
2	*, /, %	Arithmetic	Multiplication, division, and remainder
3	+, -	Arithmetic	Addition and subtraction
	+	String	String concatenation
4	<<	Integral	Left shift
	>>	Integral	Arithmetic right shift

Precedence	Operator	Type (s)	Operation Performed
	`>>>`	Integral	Logical right shift
5	`<, <=`	Arithmetic	Less than and less than or equal to
	`>, >=`	Arithmetic	Greater than and greater than or equal to
	`instanceof`	Object	Type comparison
6	`==`	Primitive	Equal
	`!=`	Primitive	Not equal
	`==`	Object	Equal
	`!=`	Object	Not equal
7	`&`	Integral	Bitwise AND
	`&`	Boolean	Boolean AND
8	`^`	Integral	Bitwise XOR
	`^`	Boolean	Boolean XOR
9	`|`	Integral	Bitwise OR
	`|`	Boolean	Boolean OR
10	`&&`	Boolean	Conditional AND
11	`||`	Boolean	Conditional OR
12	`?:`	Boolean, any, any	Conditional (ternary)
13	`= , *= , /= , %= , += , -= , <<= , >>= , >>>= , &= , ^= , |=`	Variable, any	Assignment with operator

For more information about operators, see Chapter 10 in *Java Programming For Dummies*.

Primitive Data Types

Java supports eight different primitive data types. Java strictly defines the implementation of the data types to help simplify the language and achieve platform independence. Java also guarantees default values for all variable types at the class level; the compiler won't be happy if you rely on those default values for method-local variables. If you forget to initialize method variables, the compiler reminds you every time.

The size of each data type isn't dependent on the environment as it is in other languages, such as C.

The following table lists all the data types supported in Java:

Type (Description)	Size	Default	Min Value / Max Value
boolean (True or false)	1 bit	False	
char (Unicode character)	16 bits	\u0000	\u0000 \uFFFF
byte (Signed integer)	8 bits	0	-128 127
short (Signed integer)	16 bits	0	-32768 32767
int (Signed integer)	32 bits	0	-2147483648 2147483647
long (Signed integer)	64 bits	0	-9223372036854775808 9223372036854775807
float (IEEE 754 floating-point)	32 bits	0.0	+/-3.40282347E+38 +/-1.40239846E-45
double (IEEE 754 floating-point)	64 bits	0.0	+/-1.79769313486231570E+308 +/-4.94065645841246544E-324

All integer numeric types (the 8-bit byte, 16-bit short, 32-bit int, and 64-bit long described in the table) are two's complement signed integers. Java offers no unsigned data types, but the language does add the >>> operator to perform unsigned (logical) right shift.

C programmers should be on the lookout for the following when working with data types in Java:

✦ The data type char is for single characters. Character data in Java is slightly different than that of C. Java uses the Unicode character set standard. The Unicode standard char is a 16-bit unsigned character rather than the 8-bit ASCII char used by C. Use the byte primitive data type if you want an 8-bit value.

✦ The boolean data type may only take on the values *true* or *false*.

✦ Strings in Java are objects and are not null-terminated arrays of characters as in C or C++. Strings are an instance of the java.lang.String class.

Reserving Keywords

Java reserves many words for various uses. You can't use any of these words as variable names, methods names, or any other identifier. For example, you can't declare a variable called default; you'd need to declare the variable something like defaultValue.

In the following list, we proudly present the Java reserved keywords you've searched for, but thought you'd never find.

Note: Items marked by an asterisk (*) — byvalue, cast, const, future, generic, goto, inner, operator, outer, rest, and var — are reserved but currently not used. Can you believe the nerve?

abstract	float	private
boolean	for	protected
break	future*	public
byte	generic*	rest*
byvalue*	goto*	return
case	if	short
cast*	implements	static
catch	import	super
char	inner*	switch
class	instanceof	synchronized
const*	int	this
continue	interface	throw
default	long	throws
do	native	transient
double	new	try
else	null	var*
extends	operator*	void
final	outer*	volatile
finally	package	while

You C programmers may think that true and false are reserved keywords, but they are actually boolean literals. Those sneaky Java creators fooled you again.

The Java Core API

Part III focuses on the Java core API, a collection of many classes written for you by the creators of Java. For each package of the core API, we show you a hierarchy diagram that outlines the relationship of all classes in that package. Following the diagram is a list of all the classes, contained methods, variables, and fields along with a summary and explanation. All identifiers in each class are shown in bold to make it easier for you to spot them.

The hierarchy diagrams in this part may prove essential when you write a Java program. The diagrams give you the "big picture" of what is really happening in a package. At 3:00 a.m., after 13 hours of solid programming, you may appreciate a bird's-eye view of the situation. In fact, we found ourselves consulting this part frequently before we even finished writing it.

We only have so much space in this book. We can't show you every package in the 1.1 Version of the JDK. We show the eleven most commonly used packages so that you can concentrate on just the stuff you really need to know.

In this part . . .

- ✔ java.applet **package**
- ✔ java.awt **package**
- ✔ java.awt.datatransfer **package**
- ✔ java.awt.event **package**
- ✔ java.awt.image **package**
- ✔ java.io **package**
- ✔ java.lang **package**
- ✔ java.net **package**
- ✔ java.sql **package**
- ✔ java.util **package**
- ✔ java.util.zip **package**

The java.applet Package

The java.applet package contains the Applet class, which is the superclass of all applets. Three interfaces are used in conjunction with the Applet class.

The following figure shows the class hierarchy of the applet package:

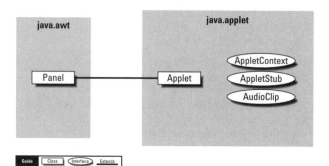

 If you want to create an applet that can run inside a Web browser, extend the Applet class and fill in the init(), start(), stop(), and destroy() methods. You don't have to use all of these methods; take a look at Chapter 2 of *Java Programming For Dummies* for the details.

java.applet.Applet

Applet is the superclass of all applets. To create an applet you must *extend* (subclass) Applet. Applet contains many useful methods for accessing data from the Web server serving the applet, such as getImage() and getAudioClip().

Applets are subject to security restrictions. See "Understanding Applet Security" in Part I for more information.

 Some of the methods listed here, such as init(), start(), stop(), and destroy(), are meant to be overridden. Part III of *Java Programming For Dummies* can give you some details on these methods.

An instance of Applet requires a stub in order to function correctly. This stub is normally provided by a Web browser or the appletviewer.

 Don't create an instance of Applet directly unless you know what you are doing — if not handled properly, methods such as getImage() won't work.

```
public class Applet extends Panel
// Instance Methods
    public void destroy()
    public AppletContext getAppletContext()
    public String getAppletInfo()
    public AudioClip getAudioClip(URL url)
    public AudioClip getAudioClip(URL url, String name)
    public URL getCodeBase()
    public URL getDocumentBase()
    public Image getImage(URL url)
    public Image getImage(URL url, String name)
    public Locale getLocale()
    public String getParameter(String name)
    public String[][] getParameterInfo()
    public void init()
    public boolean isActive()
    public void play(URL url)
    public void play(URL url, String name)
    public void resize(int width, int height)
    public void resize(Dimension d)
    public final void setStub(AppletStub stub)
    public void showStatus(String msg)
    public void start()
    public void stop()
```

java.applet.AppletContext

AppletContext defines methods used by an applet to obtain information from the applet's environment, which is usually a Web browser or the appletviewer. Don't access these methods directly; use the equivalent methods in the Applet class instead.

```
public interface AppletContext
// Instance Methods
    Applet getApplet(String name);
    Enumeration getApplets();
    AudioClip getAudioClip(URL url);
    Image getImage(URL url);
    void showDocument(URL url);
    public void showDocument(URL url, String target);
    void showStatus(String status);
```

java.applet.AppletStub

This interface gets information from the Web browser. Don't access these methods directly; use the equivalent ones in Applet instead.

```
public interface AppletStub
// Instance Methods
    void appletResize(int width, int height);
    AppletContext getAppletContext();
    URL getCodeBase();
    URL getDocumentBase();
    String getParameter(String name);
    boolean isActive();
```

java.applet.AudioClip

This interface is a simple implementation of an audio clip. The interface defines the methods that all audio clips must implement, such as `play()`, `loop()`, and `stop()`. The `Applet.getAudioClip()` method returns an `AudioClip` object.

```
public interface AudioClip
// Instance Methods
    void loop();
    void play();
    void stop();
```

The java.awt Package

The `java.awt` (Abstract Windowing Toolkit, or AWT) package contains classes for developing graphical user interfaces (GUIs).

The following figures show a class hierarchy of the `java.awt` package:

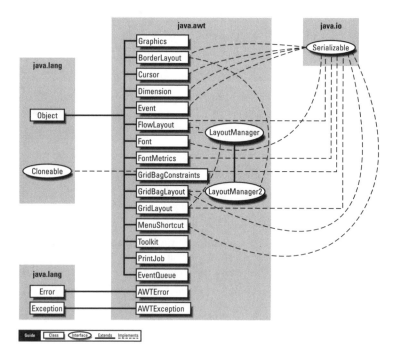

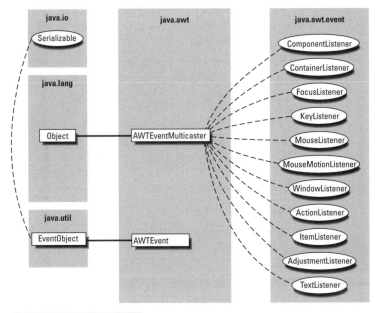

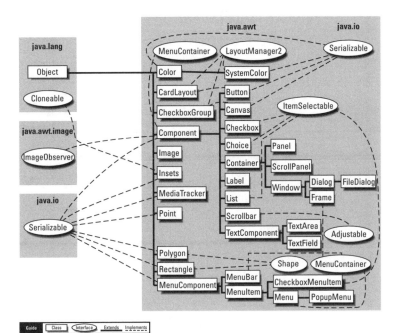

The AWT in JDK Version 1.1 contains many enhancements and also solves major AWT deficiencies that existed in JDK 1.02. The AWT enhancements include the following:

+ Richer infrastructure for larger-scale GUI development, like a spreadsheet program

+ APIs for printing and easier/faster scrolling

+ Pop-up menus

+ A clipboard for copying and pasting

+ Cursors per component

+ Delegation-based event model

+ Graphics enhancements

+ Flexible font support for internationalization

TIP

JDK 1.1 does maintain backward compatibility with the 1.0 API.

Note that separate packages exist in JDK 1.1 for java.awt.datatransfer, java.awt.event, and java.awt.image. These packages contain classes for clipboard operations, event handling, and image manipulation, respectively.

java.awt.AWTEvent

This is the top level class for events. This class and its subclasses supercede the original java.awt.Event class.

```
public abstract class AWTEvent extends EventObject
    protected int id;
    protected boolean consumed;
    public final static long COMPONENT_EVENT_MASK;
    public final static long CONTAINER_EVENT_MASK;
    public final static long FOCUS_EVENT_MASK;
    public final static long KEY_EVENT_MASK;
    public final static long MOUSE_EVENT_MASK;
    public final static long MOUSE_MOTION_EVENT_MASK;
    public final static long WINDOW_EVENT_MASK;
    public final static long ACTION_EVENT_MASK;
    public final static long ADJUSTMENT_EVENT_MASK;
    public final static long ITEM_EVENT_MASK;
    public final static int  RESERVED_ID_MAX;
    public final static long TEXT_EVENT_MASK;
    public AWTEvent(Event event)
    public AWTEvent(Object source, int id)
    protected void consume()
    Event convertToOld()
    public int getID()
    int getOldEventKey(KeyEvent e)
    protected boolean isConsumed()
    public String paramString()
    public String toString()
```

java.awt.AWTEventMulticaster

This class dispatches events to several event listeners. You register the listeners by calling the appropriate add( ) method. The events are sent when the associated method is called. For example, to send a key press event, use the keyPressed( ) method.

```
public class AWTEventMulticaster implements ComponentListener,
ContainerListener, FocusListener, KeyListener, MouseListener,
MouseMotionListener, WindowListener, ActionListener,
ItemListener, AdjustmentListener, TextListener

    protected EventListener a, b;
    public void actionPerformed(ActionEvent e)
    public static ComponentListener add(ComponentListener a,
        ComponentListener b)
    public static ContainerListener add(ContainerListener a,
        ContainerListener b)
    public static FocusListener add(FocusListener a,
        FocusListener b)
    public static KeyListener add(KeyListener a, KeyListener b)
    public static MouseListener add(MouseListener a,
        MouseListener b)
    public static MouseMotionListener add(MouseMotionListener a,
        MouseMotionListener b)
    public static WindowListener add(WindowListener a,
        WindowListener b)
    public static ActionListener add(ActionListener a,
        ActionListener b)
    public static ItemListener add(ItemListener a, ItemListener
        b)
    public static AdjustmentListener add(AdjustmentListener a,
        AdjustmentListener b)
    public static TextListener add(TextListener a, TextListener
        b)
    protected static EventListener addInternal(EventListener a,
        EventListener b)
    public void adjustmentValueChanged(AdjustmentEvent e)
    protected AWTEventMulticaster(EventListener a, EventListener
        b)
    public void componentAdded(ContainerEvent e)
    public void componentHidden(ComponentEvent e)
    public void componentMoved(ComponentEvent e)
    public void componentRemoved(ContainerEvent e)
    public void componentResized(ComponentEvent e)
    public void componentShown(ComponentEvent e)
    public void focusGained(FocusEvent e)
    public void focusLost(FocusEvent e)
    public void itemStateChanged(ItemEvent e)
    public void keyPressed(KeyEvent e)
    public void keyReleased(KeyEvent e)
    public void keyTyped(KeyEvent e)
    public void mouseClicked(MouseEvent e)
    public void mouseDragged(MouseEvent e)
    public void mouseEntered(MouseEvent e)
```

(continued)

(continued)

```
public void mouseExited(MouseEvent e)
public void mouseMoved(MouseEvent e)
public void mousePressed(MouseEvent e)
public void mouseReleased(MouseEvent e)
protected EventListener remove(EventListener oldl)
public static ComponentListener remove(ComponentListener l,
    ComponentListener oldl)
public static ContainerListener remove(ContainerListener l,
    ContainerListener oldl)
public static FocusListener remove(FocusListener l,
    FocusListener oldl)
public static KeyListener remove(KeyListener l, KeyListener
    oldl)
public static MouseListener remove(MouseListener l,
    MouseListener oldl)
public static MouseMotionListener remove(MouseMotionListener
    l, MouseMotionListener oldl)
public static WindowListener remove(WindowListener l,
    WindowListener oldl)
public static ActionListener remove(ActionListener l,
    ActionListener oldl)
public static ItemListener remove(ItemListener l,
    ItemListener oldl)
public static AdjustmentListener remove(AdjustmentListener
    l, AdjustmentListener oldl)
public static TextListener remove(TextListener l,
    TextListener oldl)
protected static EventListener removeInternal(EventListener
    l, EventListener oldl)
public void textValueChanged(TextEvent e)
public void windowActivated(WindowEvent e)
public void windowClosed(WindowEvent e)
public void windowClosing(WindowEvent e)
public void windowDeactivated(WindowEvent e)
public void windowDeiconified(WindowEvent e)
public void windowIconified(WindowEvent e)
public void windowOpened(WindowEvent e)
```

java.awt.Adjustable

Use this interface with components that can be adjusted, such as a scroll bar.

```
public interface Adjustable
    public static final int HORIZONTAL;
    public static final int VERTICAL;
    void addAdjustmentListener(AdjustmentListener l);
    int getBlockIncrement();
    int getMaximum();
    int getMinimum();
    int getOrientation();
    int getUnitIncrement();
    int getValue();
    int getVisibleAmount();
```

```
void removeAdjustmentListener(AdjustmentListener l);
void setBlockIncrement(int b);
void setMaximum(int max);
void setMinimum(int min);
void setUnitIncrement(int u);
void setValue(int v);
void setVisibleAmount(int v);
```

java.awt.BorderLayout

BorderLayout is a layout manager with five areas for adding components: North, East, West, South, and Center. The String argument to the add() method for containers specifies in which area a component should be added. If you don't specify an area, Center becomes the default. The size of each area depends on the preferred size of the components in an area. Center takes up any remaining area. Only one component can be added to an area. If you want to put more than one component in an area, add a Panel with the components inside.

```
public class BorderLayout implements LayoutManager2,
java.io.Serializable
    int hgap;
    int vgap;
    Component north;
    Component west;
    Component east;
    Component south;
    Component center;
    public static final String NORTH;
    public static final String SOUTH;
    public static final String EAST;
    public static final String WEST;
    public static final String CENTER;
    public void addLayoutComponent(Component comp, Object
        constraints)
    public void addLayoutComponent(String name, Component comp)
    public BorderLayout()
    public BorderLayout(int hgap, int vgap)
    public int getHgap()
    public float getLayoutAlignmentX(Container parent)
    public float getLayoutAlignmentY(Container parent)
    public int getVgap()
    public void invalidateLayout(Container target)
    public void layoutContainer(Container target)
    public Dimension maximumLayoutSize(Container target)
    public Dimension minimumLayoutSize(Container target)
    public Dimension preferredLayoutSize(Container target)
    public void removeLayoutComponent(Component comp)
    public void setHgap(int hgap)
    public void setVgap(int vgap)
    public String toString()
```

java.awt.Button

Button is a simple push-button component. You must add Button to a container, such as Panel or Frame, for it to be useful.

```
public class Button extends Component
    String label;
    String actionCommand;
    ActionListener actionListener;
    public void addActionListener(ActionListener l)
    public void addNotify()
    public Button()
    public Button(String label)
    boolean eventEnabled(AWTEvent e)
    public String getActionCommand()
    public String getLabel()
    protected String paramString()
    protected void processActionEvent(ActionEvent e)
    protected void processEvent(AWTEvent e)
    public void removeActionListener(ActionListener l)
    public void setActionCommand(String command)
    public synchronized void setLabel(String label)
```

java.awt.Canvas

Canvas is a rectangular area commonly used for drawing or building custom components. Canvas resembles Panel, but you can't add components to a Canvas like you can with Panel. This is because Panel is a container, meaning it can hold other components, and Canvas is not. (See "java.awt.Panel" in this part for more information on Panel.)

```
public class Canvas extends Component
    public void addNotify()
    public Canvas()
    public void paint(Graphics g)
    boolean postsOldMouseEvents()
```

java.awt.CardLayout

CardLayout lets you show one Component or Panel at a time, much like a fanned deck of cards (thus the name), saving you valuable screen space. To use CardLayout, just create a bunch of Panels with components inside and add them to a container along with a String to give the Panels unique names. If you want to show a particular Panel, just call the show() method with the name of the Panel.

```
public class CardLayout implements LayoutManager2,
java.io.Serializable
    Hashtable tab;
    int hgap;
    int vgap;
    public void addLayoutComponent(Component comp, Object
        constraints)
    public void addLayoutComponent(String name, Component comp)
    public CardLayout()
    public CardLayout(int hgap, int vgap)
    void checkLayout(Container parent)
    public void first(Container parent)
    public int getHgap()
```

```
public float getLayoutAlignmentX(Container parent)
public float getLayoutAlignmentY(Container parent)
public int getVgap()
public void invalidateLayout(Container target)
public void last(Container parent)
public void layoutContainer(Container parent)
public Dimension maximumLayoutSize(Container target)
public Dimension minimumLayoutSize(Container parent)
public void next(Container parent)
public Dimension preferredLayoutSize(Container parent)
public void previous(Container parent)
public void removeLayoutComponent(Component comp)
public void setHgap(int hgap)
public void setVgap(int vgap)
public void show(Container parent, String name)
public String toString()
```

java.awt.Checkbox

Checkbox creates a simple on/off check box. Check boxes act
independently by default. If you want to make several check boxes
mutually exclusive, what Mac users call *radio buttons,* you need to
create a CheckboxGroup (see "java.awt.CheckboxGroup" in this
part for the details on creating radio buttons).

```
public class Checkbox extends Component implements ItemSelectable
    String label;
    boolean state;
    CheckboxGroup group;
    ItemListener itemListener;
    public void addItemListener(ItemListener l)
    public void addNotify()
    public Checkbox()
    public Checkbox(String label)
    public Checkbox(String label, boolean state)
    public Checkbox(String label, boolean state, CheckboxGroup
        group)
    public Checkbox(String label, CheckboxGroup group, boolean
        state)
    boolean eventEnabled(AWTEvent e)
    public CheckboxGroup getCheckboxGroup()
    public String getLabel()
    public Object[] getSelectedObjects()
    public boolean getState()
    protected String paramString()
    protected void processEvent(AWTEvent e)
    protected void processItemEvent(ItemEvent e)
    public void removeItemListener(ItemListener l)
    public void setCheckboxGroup(CheckboxGroup g)
    public synchronized void setLabel(String label)
    public void setState(boolean state)
    synchronized void setStateInternal(boolean state)
```

java.awt. CheckboxGroup

CheckboxGroup creates groups of mutually exclusive Checkboxes, which are called *radio buttons* in the Mac world. CheckboxGroup isn't hard to use. Just create an instance of CheckboxGroup and refer to it when you create each of your Checkboxes. That way, only one of the grouped Checkboxes can be on at a time.

```
public class CheckboxGroup implements java.io.Serializable
    Checkbox selectedCheckbox;
    public CheckboxGroup()
    public Checkbox getCurrent()
    public Checkbox getSelectedCheckbox()
    public synchronized void setCurrent(Checkbox box)
    public synchronized void setSelectedCheckbox(Checkbox box)
    public String toString()
```

java.awt. CheckboxMenuItem

This class creates a MenuItem with a check box inside it. When you select this item from a menu, the check box state changes. Otherwise, it behaves like a regular MenuItem.

```
public class CheckboxMenuItem extends MenuItem implements
ItemSelectable
    boolean state;
    ItemListener itemListener;
    public void addItemListener(ItemListener l)
    public void addNotify()
    public CheckboxMenuItem()
    public CheckboxMenuItem(String label)
    public CheckboxMenuItem(String label, boolean state)
    boolean eventEnabled(AWTEvent e)
    public synchronized Object[] getSelectedObjects()
    public boolean getState()
    public String paramString()
    protected void processEvent(AWTEvent e)
    protected void processItemEvent(ItemEvent e)
    public void removeItemListener(ItemListener l)
    public synchronized void setState(boolean b)
```

java.awt. Choice

Choice is a like a pop-up menu — you can select only one of the choices at a time.

```
public class Choice extends Component implements ItemSelectable
    Vector pItems;
    int selectedIndex;
    ItemListener itemListener;
    public synchronized void add(String item)
    public synchronized void addItem(String item)
    public void addItemListener(ItemListener l)
    public void addNotify()
    public Choice()
    public int countItems()
```

```
boolean eventEnabled(AWTEvent e)
public String getItem(int index)
public int getItemCount()
public int getSelectedIndex()
public synchronized String getSelectedItem()
public synchronized Object[] getSelectedObjects()
public synchronized void insert(String item, int index)
protected String paramString()
protected void processEvent(AWTEvent e)
protected void processItemEvent(ItemEvent e)
public synchronized void remove(String item)
public synchronized void remove(int position)
public synchronized void removeAll()
public void removeItemListener(ItemListener l)
public synchronized void select(int pos)
public synchronized void select(String str)
```

java.awt.Color

`Color` is an object that can hold a 32-bit color value representing 8-bit values for red, green, blue, and alpha. You can create a `Color` with integer or floating point values. The integer values range from 0 to 255, whereas the floating point values range from 0.0 to 1.0.

```
public class Color implements java.io.Serializable
    public final static Color white;
    public final static Color lightGray;
    public final static Color gray;
    public final static Color darkGray;
    public final static Color black;
    public final static Color red;
    public final static Color pink;
    public final static Color orange;
    public final static Color yellow;
    public final static Color green;
    public final static Color magenta;
    public final static Color cyan;
    public final static Color blue;
    transient private int pData;
    int value;
    private static final double FACTOR;
    public Color brighter()
    public Color(int r, int g, int b)
    public Color(int rgb)
    public Color(float r, float g, float b)
    public Color darker()
    public static Color decode(String nm) throws
        NumberFormatException
    public boolean equals(Object obj)
    public int getBlue()
    public static Color getColor(String nm)
    public static Color getColor(String nm, Color v)
    public static Color getColor(String nm, int v)
    public int getGreen()
    public static Color getHSBColor(float h, float s, float b)
    public int getRed()
    public int getRGB()
    public int hashCode()
```

(continued)

(continued)

```
public static int HSBtoRGB(float hue, float saturation,
   float brightness)
public static float[] RGBtoHSB(int r, int g, int b, float[]
   hsbvals)
public String toString()
```

java.awt. Component

Component is the top level object in the AWT — that's why it has so much stuff in it. Many of the classes in AWT inherit from Component, such as Button, Checkbox, TextField, and so on. Containers, including Panel and Frame, are also Components, but they can hold Components as well.

Component is an abstract class, so you can't create an instance of it directly. If you want to make your own component, you should extend Canvas or Panel.

```
public abstract class Component implements ImageObserver,
MenuContainer, Serializable
         transient ComponentPeer peer;
         transient Container parent;
         int x;
         int y;
         int width;
         int height;
         Color foreground;
         Color background;
         Font font;
         Cursor cursor;
         protected Locale locale;
         boolean visible;
         boolean enabled;
         boolean valid;
         Vector popups;
         String name;
         public static final Object LOCK;
         Dimension minSize;
         Dimension prefSize;
         boolean newEventsOnly;
         ComponentListener componentListener;
         FocusListener focusListener;
         KeyListener keyListener;
         MouseListener mouseListener;
         MouseMotionListener mouseMotionListener;
         long eventMask;
         static boolean isInc;
         static int incRate;
         public static final float TOP_ALIGNMENT;
         public static final float CENTER_ALIGNMENT;
         public static final float BOTTOM_ALIGNMENT;
         public static final float LEFT_ALIGNMENT;
         public static final float RIGHT_ALIGNMENT;
         public boolean action(Event evt, Object what)
         public synchronized void add(PopupMenu popup)
         public synchronized void addComponentListener
            (ComponentListener l)
```

```
public synchronized void addFocusListener(FocusListener l)
public synchronized void addKeyListener(KeyListener l)
public synchronized void addMouseListener(MouseListener l)
public synchronized void addMouseMotionListener
   (MouseMotionListener l)
public void addNotify()
public Rectangle bounds()
public int checkImage(Image image, ImageObserver observer)
public int checkImage(Image image, int width, int height,
   ImageObserver observer)
protected Component()
public boolean contains(int x, int y)
public boolean contains(Point p)
public Image createImage(ImageProducer producer)
public Image createImage(int width, int height)
public void deliverEvent(Event e)
public void disable()
protected final void disableEvents(long eventsToDisable)
public final void dispatchEvent(AWTEvent e)
public void doLayout()
public void enable()
public void enable(boolean b)
protected final void enableEvents(long eventsToEnable)
boolean eventEnabled(AWTEvent e)
public float getAlignmentX()
public float getAlignmentY()
public Color getBackground()
public Rectangle getBounds()
public ColorModel getColorModel()
public Component getComponentAt(int x, int y)
public Component getComponentAt(Point p)
public Cursor getCursor()
public Font getFont()
public FontMetrics getFontMetrics(Font font)
public Color getForeground()
public Graphics getGraphics()
public Locale getLocale()
public Point getLocation()
public Point getLocationOnScreen()
public Dimension getMaximumSize()
public Dimension getMinimumSize()
public String getName()
Container getNativeContainer()
public Container getParent()
public ComponentPeer getPeer()
public Dimension getPreferredSize()
public Dimension getSize()
public Toolkit getToolkit()
public final Object getTreeLock()
public boolean gotFocus(Event evt, Object what)
public boolean handleEvent(Event evt)
public void hide()
public boolean imageUpdate(Image img, int flags, int x, int
   y, int w, int h)
public boolean inside(int x, int y)
public void invalidate()
public boolean isEnabled()
public boolean isFocusTraversable()
public boolean isShowing()
public boolean isValid()
public boolean isVisible()
public boolean keyDown(Event evt, int key)
```

(continued)

(continued)

```
public boolean keyUp(Event evt, int key)
public void layout()
public void list()
public void list(PrintStream out)
public void list(PrintStream out, int indent)
public void list(PrintWriter out)
public void list(PrintWriter out, int indent)
public Component locate(int x, int y)
public Point location()
public boolean lostFocus(Event evt, Object what)
public Dimension minimumSize()
public boolean mouseDown(Event evt, int x, int y)
public boolean mouseDrag(Event evt, int x, int y)
public boolean mouseEnter(Event evt, int x, int y)
public boolean mouseExit(Event evt, int x, int y)
public boolean mouseMove(Event evt, int x, int y)
public boolean mouseUp(Event evt, int x, int y)
public void move(int x, int y)
public void nextFocus()
public void paint(Graphics g)
public void paintAll(Graphics g)
protected String paramString()
public boolean postEvent(Event e)
boolean postsOldMouseEvents()
public Dimension preferredSize()
public boolean prepareImage(Image image, ImageObserver
    observer)
public boolean prepareImage(Image image, int width, int
    height, ImageObserver observer)
public void print(Graphics g)
public void printAll(Graphics g)
protected void processComponentEvent(ComponentEvent e)
protected void processEvent(AWTEvent e)
protected void processFocusEvent(FocusEvent e)
protected void processKeyEvent(KeyEvent e)
protected void processMouseEvent(MouseEvent e)
protected void processMouseMotionEvent(MouseEvent e)
public synchronized void remove(MenuComponent popup)
public synchronized void removeComponentListener
    (ComponentListener l)
public synchronized void removeFocusListener(FocusListener
    l)
public synchronized void removeKeyListener(KeyListener l)
public synchronized void removeMouseListener(MouseListener
    l)
public synchronized void removeMouseMotionListener
    (MouseMotionListener l)
public void removeNotify()
public void repaint()
public void repaint(long tm)
public void repaint(int x, int y, int width, int height)
public void repaint(long tm, int x, int y, int width, int
    height)
public void requestFocus()
public void reshape(int x, int y, int width, int height)
public void resize(int width, int height)
public void resize(Dimension d)
public void setBackground(Color c)
public void setBounds(int x, int y, int width, int height)
public void setBounds(Rectangle r)
```

```
public synchronized void setCursor(Cursor cursor)
public void setEnabled(boolean b)
public synchronized void setFont(Font f)
public void setForeground(Color c)
public void setLocale(Locale l)
public void setLocation(int x, int y)
public void setLocation(Point p)
public void setName(String name)
public void setSize(int width, int height)
public void setSize(Dimension d)
public void setVisible(boolean b)
public void show()
public void show(boolean b)
public Dimension size()
public String toString()
public void transferFocus()
public void update(Graphics g)
public void validate()
```

java.awt.Container

Container is an abstract class used for holding Components.
Panels and Frames are Containers, but Buttons and
Checkboxes are not. You can't create an instance of Container
directly; you have to subclass it if you want to use it. Most pro-
grammers use the containers provided in the API (Panel, Frame,
Dialog, and so on) and don't create their own.

```
public abstract class Container extends Component

    int ncomponents;
    Component component[];
    LayoutManager layoutMgr;
    private LightweightDispatcher dispatcher;
    private Dimension maxSize;
    ContainerListener containerListener;
    private int containerSerializedDataVersion;
    public Component add(Component comp)
    public Component add(String name, Component comp)
    public Component add(Component comp, int index)
    public void add(Component comp, Object constraints)
    public void add(Component comp, Object constraints, int
        index)
    public void addContainerListener(ContainerListener l)
    protected void addImpl(Component comp, Object constraints,
        int index)
    public void addNotify()
    protected Container()
    public int countComponents()
    public void deliverEvent(Event e)
    void dispatchEvent(AWTEvent e)
    public void doLayout()
    boolean eventEnabled(AWTEvent e)
    public float getAlignmentX()
    public float getAlignmentY()
    public Component getComponent(int n)
    public Component getComponentAt(int x, int y)
    public Component getComponentAt(Point p)
    public int getComponentCount()
```

(continued)

(continued)

```
public Component[] getComponents()
public Insets getInsets()
public LayoutManager getLayout()
public Dimension getMaximumSize()
public Dimension getMinimumSize()
Component getMouseEventTarget(int x, int y)
public Dimension getPreferredSize()
public Insets insets()
public void invalidate()
public boolean isAncestorOf(Component c)
public void layout()
public void list(PrintStream out, int indent)
public void list(PrintWriter out, int indent)
public Component locate(int x, int y)
public Dimension minimumSize()
void nextFocus(Component base)
public void paint(Graphics g)
public void paintComponents(Graphics g)
protected String paramString()
void postProcessKeyEvent(KeyEvent e)
boolean postsOldMouseEvents()
public Dimension preferredSize()
public void print(Graphics g)
public void printComponents(Graphics g)
protected void processContainerEvent(ContainerEvent e)
protected void processEvent(AWTEvent e)
void proxyEnableEvents(long events)
void proxyRequestFocus(Component c)
private void readObject(java.io.ObjectInputStream s) throws
    java.lang.ClassNotFoundException, java.io.IOException
public void remove(int index)
public void remove(Component comp)
public void removeAll()
public void removeContainerListener(ContainerListener l)
public void removeNotify()
void setFocusOwner(Component c)
public void setLayout(LayoutManager mgr)
void transferFocus(Component base)
public void validate()
protected void validateTree()
private void writeObject(java.io.ObjectOutputStream s)
    throws java.lang.ClassNotFoundException, java.io.IOException
```

java.awt.Cursor

Cursor represents a mouse cursor. You can specify cursors for
each Component using the JDK Version 1.1. Just call
Component.setCursor() with the cursor you want.

```
public class Cursor implements java.io.Serializable
    public static final int DEFAULT_CURSOR;
    public static final int CROSSHAIR_CURSOR;
    public static final int TEXT_CURSOR;
    public static final int WAIT_CURSOR;
    public static final int SW_RESIZE_CURSOR;
    public static final int SE_RESIZE_CURSOR;
    public static final int NW_RESIZE_CURSOR;
    public static final int NE_RESIZE_CURSOR;
    public static final int N_RESIZE_CURSOR;
    public static final int S_RESIZE_CURSOR;
```

```
public static final int W_RESIZE_CURSOR;
public static final int E_RESIZE_CURSOR;
public static final int HAND_CURSOR;
public static final int MOVE_CURSOR;
protected static Cursor predefined[];
int type;
public Cursor(int type)
static public Cursor getDefaultCursor()
static public Cursor getPredefinedCursor(int type)
public int getType()
```

java.awt.Dialog

Dialog lets you create a modal or modeless dialog box; a boolean flag in the constructor describes which type. You must specify a parent frame when creating a dialog box. This can be any Frame in an application.

```
public class Dialog extends Window
    boolean resizable;
    boolean modal;
    String title;
    WindowListener windowListener;
    public void addNotify()
    public Dialog(Frame parent)
    public Dialog(Frame parent, boolean modal)
    public Dialog(Frame parent, String title)
    public Dialog(Frame parent, String title, boolean modal)
    boolean eventEnabled(AWTEvent e)
    public String getTitle()
    public boolean isModal()
    public boolean isResizable()
    protected String paramString()
    protected void processEvent(AWTEvent e)
    protected void processWindowEvent(WindowEvent e)
    public void setModal(boolean b)
    public synchronized void setResizable(boolean resizable)
    public synchronized void setTitle(String title)
    public void show()
```

java.awt.Dimension

Dimension is a wrapper for width and height. Dimension objects appear all over the place for specifying width and height.

```
public class Dimension implements java.io.Serializable
    public int width;
    public int height;
    public Dimension()
    public Dimension(Dimension d)
    public Dimension(int width, int height)
    public boolean equals(Object obj)
    public Dimension getSize()
    public void setSize(Dimension d)
    public void setSize(int width, int height)
    public String toString()
```

java.awt.Event

Event holds all of the information contained in a user event, such as when the user presses a key or moves the mouse. Most of the time, you receive an Event object from the run-time environment, but you can also create your own events and send them to other Components.

```java
public class Event implements java.io.Serializable
    public static final int SHIFT_MASK;
    public static final int CTRL_MASK;
    public static final int META_MASK;
    public static final int ALT_MASK;
    public static final int HOME;
    public static final int END;
    public static final int PGUP;
    public static final int PGDN;
    public static final int UP;
    public static final int DOWN;
    public static final int LEFT;
    public static final int RIGHT;
    public static final int F1;
    public static final int F2;
    public static final int F3;
    public static final int F4;
    public static final int F5;
    public static final int F6;
    public static final int F7;
    public static final int F8;
    public static final int F9;
    public static final int F10;
    public static final int F11;
    public static final int F12;
    public static final int PRINT_SCREEN;
    public static final int SCROLL_LOCK;
    public static final int CAPS_LOCK;
    public static final int NUM_LOCK;
    public static final int PAUSE;
    public static final int INSERT;
    public static final int ENTER;
    public static final int BACK_SPACE;
    public static final int TAB;
    public static final int ESCAPE;
    public static final int DELETE;
    public static final int WINDOW_DESTROY;
    public static final int WINDOW_EXPOSE;
    public static final int WINDOW_ICONIFY;
    public static final int WINDOW_DEICONIFY;
    public static final int WINDOW_MOVED;
    public static final int KEY_PRESS;
    public static final int KEY_RELEASE;
    public static final int KEY_ACTION;
    public static final int KEY_ACTION_RELEASE;
    public static final int MOUSE_DOWN;
    public static final int MOUSE_UP;
    public static final int MOUSE_MOVE;
    public static final int MOUSE_ENTER;
    public static final int MOUSE_EXIT;
    public static final int MOUSE_DRAG;
    public static final int SCROLL_LINE_UP;
    public static final int SCROLL_LINE_DOWN;
```

```
public static final int SCROLL_PAGE_UP;
public static final int SCROLL_PAGE_DOWN;
public static final int SCROLL_ABSOLUTE;
public static final int SCROLL_BEGIN;
public static final int SCROLL_END;
public static final int LIST_SELECT;
public static final int LIST_DESELECT;
public static final int ACTION_EVENT;
public static final int LOAD_FILE;
public static final int SAVE_FILE;
public static final int GOT_FOCUS;
public static final int LOST_FOCUS;
public Object target;
public long when;
public int id;
public int x;
public int y;
public int key;
public int modifiers;
public int clickCount;
public Object arg;
public Event evt;
void consume()
public boolean controlDown()
public Event(Object target, long when, int id, int x, int y,
    int key, int modifiers, Object arg)
public Event(Object target, long when, int id, int x, int y,
    int key, int modifiers)
public Event(Object target, int id, Object arg)
boolean isConsumed()
public boolean metaDown()
protected String paramString()
public boolean shiftDown()
public String toString()
public void translate(int x, int y)
```

java.awt.EventDispatchThread

EventDispatchThread is a thread that traps events and sends them to other Components.

```
class EventDispatchThread extends Thread
    EventDispatchThread(String name)
    public void run()
    public void stopDispatching()
```

java.awt.EventQueue

EventQueue is a class that queues up events before they are sent to a Component.

```
public class EventQueue
    static EventQueue theEventQueue;
    public EventQueue()
    public synchronized Object getNextEvent() throws
        InterruptedException
    public synchronized Object peekEvent()
    public synchronized Object peekEvent(int id)
    public synchronized void postEvent(Event theEvent)
    public synchronized void postEvent(AWTEvent theEvent)
```

java.awt.FileDialog

`FileDialog` creates a file-picker dialog, which significantly reduces time spent creating user interfaces. `FileDialog` is very easy to use. Just create an instance of `FileDialog`, tell it whether it is a `LOAD` or `SAVE` type, and then call `FileDialog.show()`. `FileDialog` is modal, so `show()` blocks until the user completes the activity. When it returns, you can interrogate the object to determine which file, if any, was selected.

```
public class FileDialog extends Dialog
        public static final int LOAD;
        public static final int SAVE;
        int mode;
        String dir;
        String file;
        FilenameFilter filter;
        public void addNotify()
        public FileDialog(Frame parent)
        public FileDialog(Frame parent, String title)
        public FileDialog(Frame parent, String title, int mode)
        public String getDirectory()
        public String getFile()
        public FilenameFilter getFilenameFilter()
        public int getMode()
        protected String paramString()
        boolean postsOldMouseEvents()
        public synchronized void setDirectory(String dir)
        public synchronized void setFile(String file)
        public synchronized void setFilenameFilter(FilenameFilter
            filter)
        public void setMode(int mode)
```

java.awt.FlowLayout

`FlowLayout` is the most basic layout manager. It positions components left to right, centering them as much as possible. You may find `FlowLayout` really useful for quick protoypes when sophisticated layout is not a priority.

```
public class FlowLayout implements LayoutManager,
java.io.Serializable
        public static final int LEFT;
        public static final int CENTER;
        public static final int RIGHT;
        int align;
        int hgap;
        int vgap;
        public void addLayoutComponent(String name, Component comp)
        public FlowLayout()
        public FlowLayout(int align)
        public FlowLayout(int align, int hgap, int vgap)
        public int getAlignment()
        public int getHgap()
        public int getVgap()
        public void layoutContainer(Container target)
        public Dimension minimumLayoutSize(Container target)
```

```
public Dimension preferredLayoutSize(Container target)
public void removeLayoutComponent(Component comp)
public void setAlignment(int align)
public void setHgap(int hgap)
public void setVgap(int vgap)
public String toString()
```

java.awt.Font

Font is a class describing . . . drumroll . . . fonts! Font objects are used when setting the font for a component or a graphics object in a component's Paint method.

```
public class Font implements java.io.Serializable
    public static final int PLAIN;
    public static final int BOLD;
    public static final int ITALIC;
    protected String name;
    protected int style;
    protected int size;
    transient FontPeer peer;
    public static Font decode(String str)
    public boolean equals(Object obj)
    public Font(String name, int style, int size)
    public String getFamily()
    public static Font getFont(String nm)
    public static Font getFont(String nm, Font font)
    public String getName()
    public FontPeer getPeer()
    public int getSize()
    public int getStyle()
    public int hashCode()
    public boolean isBold()
    public boolean isItalic()
    public boolean isPlain()
    public String toString()
    private void writeObject(java.io.ObjectOutputStream s)
        throws java.lang.ClassNotFoundException, java.io.IOException
```

java.awt.FontMetrics

FontMetrics gets information about a font, such as the font's height, ascent, descent, and so on. FontMetrics often comes in handy when drawing text using Graphics.drawString(). To use this class, just create a new instance with the font of interest as a parameter to the constructor.

```
public abstract class FontMetrics implements java.io.Serializable
    protected Font font;
    public int bytesWidth(byte data[], int off, int len)
    public int charsWidth(char data[], int off, int len)
    public int charWidth(int ch)
    public int charWidth(char ch)
    protected FontMetrics(Font font)
    public int getAscent()
    public int getDescent()
    public Font getFont()
    public int getHeight()
```

(continued)

(continued)

```
public int getLeading()
public int getMaxAdvance()
public int getMaxAscent()
public int getMaxDecent()
public int getMaxDescent()
public int[] getWidths()
public int stringWidth(String str)
public String toString()
```

java.awt.Frame

Frame creates a window with a title bar. You may ask: If that's all Frame is good for, why not just create a Window? Window is the superclass of Frame (and Dialog as well). You can't create an instance of Window for various reasons that are way too complicated to explain here. Just remember: When you want a standard window, use Frame, not Window. Is that confusing enough? Just trust us on this one.

TIP The default layout manager for Frame, and all Window subclasses for that matter, is BorderLayout. You should set the layout anyway, just to be certain.

```
public class Frame extends Window implements MenuContainer
        public static final int DEFAULT_CURSOR;
        public static final int CROSSHAIR_CURSOR;
        public static final int TEXT_CURSOR;
        public static final int WAIT_CURSOR;
        public static final int SW_RESIZE_CURSOR;
        public static final int SE_RESIZE_CURSOR;
        public static final int NW_RESIZE_CURSOR;
        public static final int NE_RESIZE_CURSOR;
        public static final int N_RESIZE_CURSOR;
        public static final int S_RESIZE_CURSOR;
        public static final int W_RESIZE_CURSOR;
        public static final int E_RESIZE_CURSOR;
        public static final int HAND_CURSOR;
        public static final int MOVE_CURSOR;
        String title;
        Image icon;
        MenuBar menuBar;
        boolean resizable;
        Vector ownedWindows;
        WindowListener windowListener;
        public void addNotify()
        Window addOwnedWindow(Window window)
        public synchronized void dispose()
        boolean eventEnabled(AWTEvent e)
        public Frame()
        public Frame(String title)
        public int getCursorType()
        public Image getIconImage()
        public MenuBar getMenuBar()
        public String getTitle()
        public boolean isResizable()
        protected String paramString()
        void postProcessKeyEvent(KeyEvent e)
```

```
protected void processEvent(AWTEvent e)
protected void processWindowEvent(WindowEvent e)
public synchronized void remove(MenuComponent m)
void removeOwnedWindow(Window window)
public synchronized void setCursor(int cursorType)
public synchronized void setIconImage(Image image)
public synchronized void setMenuBar(MenuBar mb)
public synchronized void setResizable(boolean resizable)
public synchronized void setTitle(String title)
```

java.awt.Graphics

The magical graphics object. You can't create a `Graphics`, because it's abstract.

If you can't create one, then how do you get one? You can get a `Graphics` in a component's paint or update method. You can also get a `Graphics` from an `Image` object by calling `Image.getGraphics`. That's useful for off-screen rendering for use with double buffering.

`Graphics` contains all of the basic drawing methods, such as `drawLine`, `drawRect`, `drawOval`, and so on.

```
public abstract class Graphics
    public abstract void clearRect(int x, int y, int width, int
        height);
    public abstract void clipRect(int x, int y, int width, int
        height);
    public abstract void copyArea(int x, int y, int width, int
        height, int dx, int dy);
    public abstract Graphics create();
    public Graphics create(int x, int y, int width, int height)
    public abstract void dispose();
    public void draw3DRect(int x, int y, int width, int height,
        boolean raised)
    public abstract void drawArc(int x, int y, int width, int
        height, int startAngle, int arcAngle);
    public void drawBytes(byte data[], int offset, int length,
        int x, int y)
    public void drawChars(char data[], int offset, int length,
        int x, int y)
    public abstract boolean drawImage(Image img, int x, int y,
        ImageObserver observer);
    public abstract boolean drawImage(Image img, int x, int y,
        int width, int height, ImageObserver observer);
    public abstract boolean drawImage(Image img, int x, int y,
        Color bgcolor, ImageObserver observer);
    public abstract boolean drawImage(Image img, int x, int y,
        int width, int height, Color bgcolor, ImageObserver
        observer);
    public abstract boolean drawImage(Image img, int dx1, int
        dy1, int dx2, int dy2, int sx1, int sy1, int sx2, int sy2,
        ImageObservdrawimage
    public abstract boolean drawImage(Image img, int dx1, int
        dy1, int dx2, int dy2, int sx1, int sy1, int sx2, int sy2,
        Color bgcoldrawimage
    public abstract void drawLine(int x1, int y1, int x2, int
        y2);
```

(continued)

(continued)

```
public abstract void drawOval(int x, int y, int width, int
    height);
public abstract void drawPolygon(int xPoints[], int
    yPoints[], int nPoints);
public void drawPolygon(Polygon p)
public abstract void drawPolyline(int xPoints[], int
    yPoints[], int nPoints);
public void drawRect(int x, int y, int width, int height)
public abstract void drawRoundRect(int x, int y, int width,
    int height, int arcWidth, int arcHeight);
public abstract void drawString(String str, int x, int y);
public void fill3DRect(int x, int y, int width, int height,
    boolean raised)
public abstract void fillArc(int x, int y, int width, int
    height, int startAngle, int arcAngle);
public abstract void fillOval(int x, int y, int width, int
    height);
public abstract void fillPolygon(int xPoints[], int
    yPoints[], int nPoints);
public void fillPolygon(Polygon p)
public abstract void fillRect(int x, int y, int width, int
    height);
public abstract void fillRoundRect(int x, int y, int width,
    int height, int arcWidth, int arcHeight);
public void finalize()
public abstract Shape getClip();
public abstract Rectangle getClipBounds();
public Rectangle getClipRect()
public abstract Color getColor();
public abstract Font getFont();
public FontMetrics getFontMetrics()
public abstract FontMetrics getFontMetrics(Font f);
protected Graphics()
public abstract void setClip(int x, int y, int width, int
    height);
public abstract void setClip(Shape clip);
public abstract void setColor(Color c);
public abstract void setFont(Font font);
public abstract void setPaintMode();
public abstract void setXORMode(Color c1);
public String toString()
public abstract void translate(int x, int y);
```

java.awt.GridBagConstraints

GridBagConstraints is used in conjunction with
GridBagLayout to set up a number of constraints for a component before the component is added to a container. Many constraints you can play with interact with each other in funny ways.
Jump in and have some fun.

GridBagLayout is not for the neophyte. Be patient and use it
when you have mastered the other layout managers first.

```
public class GridBagConstraints implements Cloneable,
java.io.Serializable

    public static final int RELATIVE;
    public static final int REMAINDER;
    public static final int NONE;
```

```
public static final int BOTH;
public static final int HORIZONTAL;
public static final int VERTICAL;
public static final int CENTER;
public static final int NORTH;
public static final int NORTHEAST;
public static final int EAST;
public static final int SOUTHEAST;
public static final int SOUTH;
public static final int SOUTHWEST;
public static final int WEST;
public static final int NORTHWEST;
public int gridx, gridy, gridwidth, gridheight;
public double weightx, weighty;
public int anchor, fill;
public Insets insets;
public int ipadx, ipady;
int tempX, tempY;
int tempWidth, tempHeight;
int minWidth, minHeight;
public Object clone()
public GridBagConstraints()
```

java.awt.GridBagLayoutInfo

GridBagLayoutInfo provides information to GridBagLayout.
GridBagLayoutInfo isn't public; you can't use it unless you are
in the awt package . . . which more or less makes it unlikely that
you will have much use for GridBagLayoutInfo.

```
class GridBagLayoutInfo implements java.io.Serializable
    int width, height;
    int startx, starty;
    int minWidth[];
    int minHeight[];
    double weightX[];
    double weightY[];
    GridBagLayoutInfo()
```

java.awt.GridBagLayout

GridBagLayout, the most flexible and most cantankerous of all
layout managers, is too complicated for us to describe effectively
here. If you master GridBagLayout, you can create some impres-
sive layouts. Use GridBagLayout with caution when you are in a
good mood.

```
public class GridBagLayout implements LayoutManager2,
java.io.Serializable
    protected static final int MAXGRIDSIZE;
    protected static final int MINSIZE;
    protected static final int PREFERREDSIZE;
    protected Hashtable comptable;
    protected GridBagConstraints defaultConstraints;
    protected GridBagLayoutInfo layoutInfo;
    public int columnWidths[];
    public int rowHeights[];
```

(continued)

(continued)

```
public double columnWeights[];
public double rowWeights[];
public void addLayoutComponent(String name, Component comp)
public void addLayoutComponent(Component comp, Object
  constraints)
protected void AdjustForGravity(GridBagConstraints con
  straints, Rectangle r)
protected void ArrangeGrid(Container parent)
public GridBagConstraints getConstraints(Component comp)
public float getLayoutAlignmentX(Container parent)
public float getLayoutAlignmentY(Container parent)
public int [][] getLayoutDimensions()
protected GridBagLayoutInfo GetLayoutInfo(Container parent,
  int sizeflag)
public Point getLayoutOrigin()
public double [][] getLayoutWeights()
protected Dimension GetMinSize(Container parent,
  GridBagLayoutInfo info)
public GridBagLayout()
public void invalidateLayout(Container target)
public void layoutContainer(Container parent)
public Point location(int x, int y)
protected GridBagConstraints lookupConstraints(Component
  comp)
public Dimension maximumLayoutSize(Container target)
public Dimension minimumLayoutSize(Container parent)
public Dimension preferredLayoutSize(Container parent)
public void removeLayoutComponent(Component comp)
public void setConstraints(Component comp,
  GridBagConstraints constraints)
public String toString()
```

java.awt.GridLayout

Use `GridLayout` when you want to position several components in a grid. To use `GridLayout`, create a `GridLayout` object with the number of rows and columns you want and then add components to the container. Add the components from left to right, and from top to bottom.

When you create a `GridLayout`, be very careful how many components you add. The layout manager tends to get upset if you don't add exactly the correct number of components. For example, if you have a 3-x-3 grid, make sure to add nine components.

```
public class GridLayout implements LayoutManager,
java.io.Serializable
    int hgap;
    int vgap;
    int rows;
    int cols;
    public void addLayoutComponent(String name, Component comp)
    public int getColumns()
    public int getHgap()
    public int getRows()
    public int getVgap()
    public GridLayout()
    public GridLayout(int rows, int cols)
```

```
public GridLayout(int rows, int cols, int hgap, int vgap)
public void layoutContainer(Container parent)
public Dimension minimumLayoutSize(Container parent)
public Dimension preferredLayoutSize(Container parent)
public void removeLayoutComponent(Component comp)
public void setColumns(int cols)
public void setHgap(int hgap)
public void setRows(int rows)
public void setVgap(int vgap)
public String toString()
```

java.awt.Image

Image is one of the reasons why Java became an instant success. Programmers first saw Image in the simple Tumbling Duke demo applet from Sun Microsystems. That demo inspired thousands of programmers by showing the world how easy it is to animate images in Java. If you haven't seen Tumbling Duke, look for it in the demos that come with the JDK.

We just show you the basic stuff here. If you want to get at the pixels of an Image, you need to look at the PixelGrabber class.

You can't create Image directly because it's abstract. Most of the time, you can get an Image from someone using getImage. You can also create an Image from raw pixel values using Component.createImage.

```
public abstract class Image implements java.io.Serializable
    public static final Object UndefinedProperty;
    public static final int SCALE_DEFAULT;
    public static final int SCALE_FAST;
    public static final int SCALE_SMOOTH;
    public static final int SCALE_REPLICATE;
    public static final int SCALE_AREA_AVERAGING;
    public Image getscaledinstance(int width, int height, int
        hints)
    public abstract void flush();
    public abstract Graphics getGraphics();
    public abstract int getHeight(ImageObserver observer);
    public abstract Object getProperty(String name,
        ImageObserver observer);
    public abstract ImageProducer getSource();
    public abstract int getWidth(ImageObserver observer);
```

java.awt.Insets

Insets is a curious little class used for adding space between components in a container. Insets often comes into play in conjunction with GridbagLayout.

```
public class Insets implements Cloneable, java.io.Serializable
    public int top;
    public int left;
    public int bottom;
    public int right;
```

(continued)

(continued)

```
public Object clone()
public boolean equals(Object obj)
public Insets(int top, int left, int bottom, int right)
public String toString()
```

java.awt.ItemSelectable

ItemSelectable is an interface used by classes that can hold one or more selectable items. The List class implements this interface.

```
public interface ItemSelectable
    public void addItemListener(ItemListener l);
    public Object[] getSelectedObjects();
    public void removeItemListener(ItemListener l);
```

java.awt.Label

Label, a Component, just displays text on a single line. You can effectively do the same thing by using Graphics.drawString, but it's a lot easier to use Label. It works like any other component — just add it to a container.

```
public class Label extends Component
    public static final int LEFT;
    public static final int CENTER;
    public static final int RIGHT;
    String text;
    int alignment;
    public void addNotify()
    public int getAlignment()
    public String getText()
    public Label()
    public Label(String text)
    public Label(String text, int alignment)
    protected String paramString()
    public synchronized void setAlignment(int alignment)
    public synchronized void setText(String text)
```

java.awt.LayoutManager

If you ever want to create your own LayoutManager, you implement this class. Otherwise, you don't really need to worry about LayoutManager. Basically, all LayoutManagers (such as FlowLayout and GridLayout) must implement this interface and fill in the methods.

```
public interface LayoutManager
    void addLayoutComponent(String name, Component comp);
    void layoutContainer(Container parent);
    Dimension minimumLayoutSize(Container parent);
    Dimension preferredLayoutSize(Container parent);
    void removeLayoutComponent(Component comp);
```

```
public synchronized boolean checkID(int id, boolean load)
public synchronized Object[] getErrorsAny()
public synchronized Object[] getErrorsID(int id)
public synchronized boolean isErrorAny()
public synchronized boolean isErrorID(int id)
public MediaTracker(Component comp)
public synchronized void removeImage(Image image)
public synchronized void removeImage(Image image, int id)
public synchronized void removeImage(Image image, int id,
    int width, int height)
synchronized void setDone()
public synchronized int statusAll(boolean load)
public synchronized int statusID(int id, boolean load)
public void waitForAll() throws InterruptedException
public synchronized boolean waitForAll(long ms) throws
    InterruptedException
public void waitForID(int id) throws InterruptedException
public synchronized boolean waitForID(int id, long ms)
    throws InterruptedException
```

java.awt.Menu

Menu is one of three classes used to create menus in a Frame.
(The other classes are MenuBar and MenuItem (or
CheckboxMenuItem)). Menus are not Components, so they can't
be added to Containers. Menus are added to MenuBars, and
MenuItems are added to Menus. Menus can also be added to
Menus to create cascaded menus.

```
public class Menu extends MenuItem implements MenuContainer
    Vector items;
    boolean tearOff;
    boolean isHelpMenu;
    public synchronized MenuItem add(MenuItem mi)
    public void add(String label)
    public void addNotify()
    public void addSeparator()
    public int countItems()
    void deleteShortcut(MenuShortcut s)
    public MenuItem getItem(int index)
    public int getItemCount()
    MenuItem getShortcutMenuItem(MenuShortcut s)
    boolean handleShortcut(KeyEvent e)
    public synchronized void insert(MenuItem menuitem, int
        index)
    public void insert(String label, int index)
    public void insertSeparator(int index)
    public boolean isTearOff()
    public Menu()
    public Menu(String label)
    public Menu(String label, boolean tearOff)
    public String paramString()
    public synchronized void remove(int index)
    public synchronized void remove(MenuComponent item)
    public synchronized void removeAll()
    public void removeNotify()
    synchronized Enumeration shortcuts()
```

java.awt.MenuBar

A Frame can hold a MenuBar, which appears in the top of a Frame. To use MenuBar, create an instance of it and add it to a Frame by calling Frame.setMenuBar.

```
public class MenuBar extends MenuComponent implements
MenuContainer
        Vector menus;
        Menu helpMenu;
        public synchronized Menu add(Menu m)
        public void addNotify()
        public int countMenus()
        public void deleteShortcut(MenuShortcut s)
        public Menu getHelpMenu()
        public Menu getMenu(int i)
        public int getMenuCount()
        public MenuItem getShortcutMenuItem(MenuShortcut s)
        boolean handleShortcut(KeyEvent e)
        public MenuBar()
        public synchronized void remove(int index)
        public synchronized void remove(MenuComponent m)
        public void removeNotify()
        public synchronized void setHelpMenu(Menu m)
        public synchronized Enumeration shortcuts()
```

java.awt.MenuComponent

MenuComponent is the superclass of Menu objects. It's abstract, and so you can't create an instance of it directly. You probably won't have to deal with MenuComponent unless you plan to create your own menu items.

```
public abstract class MenuComponent implements
java.io.Serializable
        transient MenuComponentPeer peer;
        transient MenuContainer parent;
        Font font;
        String name;
        boolean newEventsOnly;
        void dispatchEvent(AWTEvent e)
        boolean eventEnabled(AWTEvent e)
        public Font getFont()
        public String getName()
        public MenuContainer getParent()
        public MenuComponentPeer getPeer()
        protected String paramString()
        public boolean postEvent(Event evt)
        protected void processEvent(AWTEvent e)
        public void removeNotify()
        public void setFont(Font f)
        public void setName(String name)
        public String toString()
```

java.awt.MenuContainer

Welcome to MenuContainer, an interface used with Menus. Unless you want to create your own type of Menu, we're sorry to say that you won't have much use for `MenuContainer`. But take a peek at it, just in case you need it at some point.

```
public interface MenuContainer
    Font getFont();
    boolean postEvent(Event evt);
    void remove(MenuComponent comp);
```

java.awt.MenuItem

`MenuItem` creates the actual item that a user selects from a `Menu`. (See "java.awtCheckboxMenuItem" in this part if you want a `Checkbox` in your `MenuItem`.) You're in luck — `MenuItem` also supports keyboard shortcuts. To create a `MenuItem`, just create an instance of `MenuItem` and add it to a `Menu`.

```
public class MenuItem extends MenuComponent
    boolean enabled;
    String label;
    String actionCommand;
    long eventMask;
    ActionListener actionListener;
    public void addActionListener(ActionListener l)
    public void addNotify()
    public void deleteShortcut()
    void deleteShortcut(MenuShortcut s)
    public synchronized void disable()
    protected final void disableEvents(long eventsToDisable)
    public synchronized void enable()
    public void enable(boolean b)
    protected final void enableEvents(long eventsToEnable)
    boolean eventEnabled(AWTEvent e)
    public String getActionCommand()
    public String getLabel()
    public MenuShortcut getShortcut()
    MenuItem getShortcutMenuItem(MenuShortcut s)
    boolean handleShortcut(KeyEvent e)
    public boolean isEnabled()
    public MenuItem()
    public MenuItem(String label)
    public MenuItem(String label, MenuShortcut s)
    public String paramString()
    protected void processActionEvent(ActionEvent e)
    protected void processEvent(AWTEvent e)
    public void removeActionListener(ActionListener l)
    public void setActionCommand(String command)
    public synchronized void setEnabled(boolean b)
    public synchronized void setLabel(String label)
    public void setShortcut(MenuShortcut s)
```

java.awt.MenuShortcut

If you ever wondered which class creates keyboard shortcuts for `MenuItem`s, then search no further than `MenuShortcut`.

```
public class MenuShortcut implements Serializable
    public boolean equals(MenuShortcut s)
    public int getKey()
    protected String paramString()
    public String toString()
    public boolean usesShiftModifier()
```

java.awt.Panel

You can use `Panel`, a rectangular area, to draw or add
`Components`. Because `Panel` is a container, most of the time, you
use `Panel` to group `Components`. You may notice similarities
between `Panel` and `Canvas`, but `Panel` is a `Container` and
`Canvas` is not. The default layout manager for `Panel` (and all subclasses, such as `Applet`) is `FlowLayout`.

```
public class Panel extends Container
    final static LayoutManager panelLayout;
    public void addNotify()
    public Panel()
    public Panel(LayoutManager layout)
```

java.awt.Point

Sometimes you may need a simple class to hold an x and y
coordinate. Enter `Point` to do just that.

```
public class Point implements java.io.Serializable
    public int x;
    public int y;
    public boolean equals(Object obj)
    public Point getLocation()
    public int hashCode()
    public void move(int x, int y)
    public Point()
    public Point(Point p)
    public Point(int x, int y)
    public void setLocation(Point p)
    public void setLocation(int x, int y)
    public String toString()
    public void translate(int x, int y)
```

java.awt.Polygon

`Polygon` draws polygons. The `Graphics` class contains a
`drawPolygon()` method, which takes a `Polygon` object as an
argument and actually does the drawing. `Polygon` just holds the
coordinates of the vertices.

```
public class Polygon implements Shape, java.io.Serializable
    public int npoints;
    public int xpoints[];
    public int ypoints[];
    protected Rectangle bounds;
    public void addPoint(int x, int y)
```

```
void calculateBounds(int xpoints[], int ypoints[], int
    npoints)
public boolean contains(Point p)
public boolean contains(int x, int y)
public Rectangle getBoundingBox()
public Rectangle getBounds()
public boolean inside(int x, int y)
public Polygon()
public Polygon(int xpoints[], int ypoints[], int npoints)
public void translate(int deltaX, int deltaY)
void updateBounds(int x, int y)
```

java.awt.PopupMenu

PopupMenu creates a pop-up menu anywhere in a Component. To use it, just create an instance, add some MenuItems (or CheckboxMenuItems), and then call PopupMenu.show() with the Component and coordinates specifying where you want the pop-up to appear.

```
public class PopupMenu extends Menu
    public synchronized void addNotify()
    public PopupMenu()
    public PopupMenu(String label)
    public void show(Component origin, int x, int y)
```

java.awt.PrintGraphics

This interface provides a print graphics context for a page. This class contains one method for returning the PrintJob object from which the PrintGraphics object originated.

```
public interface PrintGraphics
    public PrintJob getPrintJob();
```

java.awt.PrintJob

PrintJob is used to effect printing. The class is abstract, so you instantiate it directly. You must get an instance from Toolkit using getPrintJob().

```
public abstract class PrintJob
    public abstract void end();
    public void finalize()
    public abstract Graphics getGraphics();
    public abstract Dimension getPageDimension();
    public abstract int getPageResolution();
    public abstract boolean lastPageFirst();
```

java.awt.Rectangle

Rectangle is a utility class that holds four integers: x, y, width, and height. Rectangle offers some useful methods, such as inside(), which tells you if a point is inside the Rectangle.

```
public class Rectangle implements Shape, java.io.Serializable
    public int x;
    public int y;
    public int width;
    public int height;
    public void add(int newx, int newy)
    public void add(Point pt)
    public void add(Rectangle r)
    public boolean contains(Point p)
    public boolean contains(int x, int y)
    public boolean equals(Object obj)
    public Rectangle getBounds()
    public Point getLocation()
    public Dimension getSize()
    public void grow(int h, int v)
    public int hashCode()
    public boolean inside(int x, int y)
    public Rectangle intersection(Rectangle r)
    public boolean intersects(Rectangle r)
    public boolean isEmpty()
    public void move(int x, int y)
    public Rectangle()
    public Rectangle(Rectangle r)
    public Rectangle(int x, int y, int width, int height)
    public Rectangle(int width, int height)
    public Rectangle(Point p, Dimension d)
    public Rectangle(Point p)
    public Rectangle(Dimension d)
    public void reshape(int x, int y, int width, int height)
    public void resize(int width, int height)
    public void setBounds(Rectangle r)
    public void setBounds(int x, int y, int width, int height)
    public void setLocation(Point p)
    public void setLocation(int x, int y)
    public void setSize(Dimension d)
    public void setSize(int width, int height)
    public String toString()
    public void translate(int x, int y)
    public Rectangle union(Rectangle r)
```

java.awt.ScrollPane

ScrollPane, a new Container in JDK 1.1, creates a scrollable Panel. ScrollPane that works just like a Panel (see "java.awt.Panel" in this part), except that scroll bars can be displayed and used to scroll components.

```
public class ScrollPane extends Container
    public static final int SCROLLBARS_AS_NEEDED;
    public static final int SCROLLBARS_ALWAYS;
    public static final int SCROLLBARS_NEVER;
    public Component add(Component comp, int pos)
    public void addNotify()
```

```
public void doLayout()
public Adjustable getHAdjustable()
public int getHScrollbarHeight()
public int getScrollbarDisplayPolicy()
public Point getScrollPosition()
public Adjustable getVAdjustable()
public Dimension getViewportSize()
public int getVScrollbarWidth()
public void layout()
public String paramString()
public void printComponents(Graphics g)
public ScrollPane()
public ScrollPane(int scrollbarDisplayPolicy)
public final void setLayout(LayoutManager mgr)
public void setScrollPosition(int x, int y)
public void setScrollPosition(Point p)
```

java.awt.Scrollbar

Belly up to the Scrollbar, which is a Component like Button or Checkbox. To use this class, all you have to do is create an instance and add it to a Container. You can specify page and line increments, although default values take effect if you don't.

```
public class Scrollbar extends Component implements Adjustable
    public static final int HORIZONTAL;
    public static final int VERTICAL;
    int value;
    int maximum;
    int minimum;
    int visibleAmount;
    int orientation;
    int lineIncrement;
    int pageIncrement;
    AdjustmentListener adjustmentListener;
    public void addAdjustmentListener(AdjustmentListener l)
    public void addNotify()
    boolean eventEnabled(AWTEvent e)
    public int getBlockIncrement()
    public int getLineIncrement()
    public int getMaximum()
    public int getMinimum()
    public int getOrientation()
    public int getPageIncrement()
    public int getUnitIncrement()
    public int getValue()
    public int getVisible()
    public int getVisibleAmount()
    protected String paramString()
    protected void processAdjustmentEvent(AdjustmentEvent e)
    protected void processEvent(AWTEvent e)
    public void removeAdjustmentListener(AdjustmentListener l)
    public Scrollbar()
    public Scrollbar(int orientation)
    public Scrollbar(int orientation, int value, int visible,
        int minimum, int maximum)
    public synchronized void setBlockIncrement(int v)
    public void setLineIncrement(int v)
    public synchronized void setMaximum(int newMaximum)
    public synchronized void setMinimum(int newMinimum)
```

(continued)

(continued)

```
public synchronized void setOrientation(int orientation)
public void setPageIncrement(int v)
public synchronized void setUnitIncrement(int v)
public synchronized void setValue(int newValue)
public synchronized void setValues(int value, int visible,
    int minimum, int maximum)
public synchronized void setVisibleAmount(int newAmount)
```

java.awt.Shape

Shape is an interface used by some of the graphics-related classes.

```
public interface Shape
    public Rectangle getBounds();
```

java.awt.SystemColor

SystemColor describes symbolic colors representing the color of
GUI objects on a system.

```
public final class SystemColor extends Color implements
java.io.Serializable
    public final static int DESKTOP;
    public final static int ACTIVE_CAPTION;
    public final static int ACTIVE_CAPTION_TEXT;
    public final static int ACTIVE_CAPTION_BORDER;
    public final static int INACTIVE_CAPTION;
    public final static int INACTIVE_CAPTION_TEXT;
    public final static int INACTIVE_CAPTION_BORDER;
    public final static int WINDOW;
    public final static int WINDOW_BORDER;
    public final static int WINDOW_TEXT;
    public final static int MENU;
    public final static int MENU_TEXT;
    public final static int TEXT;
    public final static int TEXT_TEXT;
    public final static int TEXT_HIGHLIGHT;
    public final static int TEXT_HIGHLIGHT_TEXT;
    public final static int TEXT_INACTIVE_TEXT;
    public final static int CONTROL;
    public final static int CONTROL_TEXT;
    public final static int CONTROL_HIGHLIGHT;
    public final static int CONTROL_LT_HIGHLIGHT;
    public final static int CONTROL_SHADOW;
    public final static int CONTROL_DK_SHADOW;
    public final static int SCROLLBAR;
    public final static int INFO;
    public final static int INFO_TEXT;
    public final static int NUM_COLORS;
    public final static SystemColor desktop;
    public final static SystemColor activeCaption;
    public final static SystemColor activeCaptionText;
    public final static SystemColor activeCaptionBorder;
    public final static SystemColor inactiveCaption;
    public final static SystemColor inactiveCaptionText;
    public final static SystemColor inactiveCaptionBorder;
    public final static SystemColor window;
    public final static SystemColor windowBorder;
    public final static SystemColor windowText;
```

```
public final static SystemColor menu;
public final static SystemColor menuText;
public final static SystemColor text;
public final static SystemColor textText;
public final static SystemColor textHighlight;
public final static SystemColor textHighlightText;
public final static SystemColor textInactiveText;
public final static SystemColor control;
public final static SystemColor controlText;
public final static SystemColor controlHighlight;
public final static SystemColor controlLtHighlight;
public final static SystemColor controlShadow;
public final static SystemColor controlDkShadow;
public final static SystemColor scrollbar;
public final static SystemColor info;
public final static SystemColor infoText;
```

java.awt.TextArea

TextArea is a multi-line area used for editing. It is a Component, so you can add it to any Container. TextArea can automatically handle key events, including cut and paste operations. This class can also create scroll bars and handle the events as expected.

Note that some of the methods you may expect to find in this class, such as getText(), are actually defined in TextComponent. If you don't find what you are looking for here, look in TextComponent (see "java.awt.TextComponent" in this part).

```
public class TextArea extends TextComponent
    int rows;
    int columns;
    public static final int SCROLLBARS_BOTH;
    public static final int SCROLLBARS_VERTICAL_ONLY;
    public static final int SCROLLBARS_HORIZONTAL_ONLY;
    public static final int SCROLLBARS_NONE;
    public void addNotify()
    public synchronized void append(String str)
    public void appendText(String str)
    public int getColumns()
    public Dimension getMinimumSize(int rows, int columns)
    public Dimension getMinimumSize()
    public Dimension getPreferredSize(int rows, int columns)
    public Dimension getPreferredSize()
    public int getRows()
    public int getScrollbarVisibility()
    public synchronized void insert(String str, int pos)
    public void insertText(String str, int pos)
    public Dimension minimumSize(int rows, int columns)
    public Dimension minimumSize()
    protected String paramString()
    public Dimension preferredSize(int rows, int columns)
    public Dimension preferredSize()
    public synchronized void replaceRange(String str, int start,
        int end)
    public void replaceText(String str, int start, int end)
    public void setColumns(int columns)
    public void setRows(int rows)
```

(continued)

(continued)

```
public TextArea()
public TextArea(String text)
public TextArea(String text, int rows, int columns)
public TextArea(String text, int rows, int columns, int
    scrollbars)
public TextArea(int rows, int columns)
```

java.awt.TextComponent

TextComponent is the superclass of TextField and TextArea.
It just factors out some of the common behavior in the two
classes.

You probably won't access this class directly, but you may have to
look here to find expected methods that don't appear in
TextField or TextArea.

```
public class TextComponent extends Component
    String text;
    boolean editable;
    int selectionStart;
    int selectionEnd;
    protected TextListener textListener;
    public void addTextListener(TextListener l)
    boolean eventEnabled(AWTEvent e)
    public int getCaretPosition()
    public synchronized String getSelectedText()
    public synchronized int getSelectionEnd()
    public synchronized int getSelectionStart()
    public synchronized String getText()
    public boolean isEditable()
    protected String paramString()
    protected void processEvent(AWTEvent e)
    protected void processTextEvent(TextEvent e)
    public void removeNotify()
    public void removeTextListener(TextListener l)
    public synchronized void select(int selectionStart, int
        selectionEnd)
    public synchronized void selectAll()
    public void setCaretPosition(int position)
    public synchronized void setEditable(boolean b)
    public synchronized void setSelectionEnd(int selectionEnd)
    public synchronized void setSelectionStart(int
        selectionStart)
    public synchronized void setText(String t)
    TextComponent(String text)
```

java.awt.TextField

TextField is a single line of editable text. You can specify the
number of columns that are visible in one of the constructors.
TextField can be made non-editable if you just want to display
text with a border around it for aesthetics.

```
public class TextField extends TextComponent
```

```
int columns;
char echoChar;
ActionListener actionListener;
public void addActionListener(ActionListener l)
public void addNotify()
public boolean echoCharIsSet()
boolean eventEnabled(AWTEvent e)
public int getColumns()
public char getEchoChar()
public Dimension getMinimumSize(int columns)
public Dimension getMinimumSize()
public Dimension getPreferredSize(int columns)
public Dimension getPreferredSize()
public Dimension minimumSize(int columns)
public Dimension minimumSize()
protected String paramString()
public Dimension preferredSize(int columns)
public Dimension preferredSize()
protected void processActionEvent(ActionEvent e)
protected void processEvent(AWTEvent e)
public void removeActionListener(ActionListener l)
public void setColumns(int columns)
public void setEchoChar(char c)
public void setEchoCharacter(char c)
public TextField()
public TextField(String text)
public TextField(String text, int columns)
public TextField(int columns)
```

java.awt.Toolkit

Toolkit is a catch-all for finding properties of a system, such as
screen size, resolution, available fonts, and so on. Because
Toolkit is abstract, you must get an instance of the object by
calling Toolkit.getDefaultToolkit().

```
public abstract class Toolkit
    public abstract void beep();
    public abstract int checkImage(Image image, int width, int
        height, ImageObserver observer);
    protected abstract ButtonPeer createButton(Button target);
    protected abstract CanvasPeer createCanvas(Canvas target);
    protected abstract CheckboxPeer createCheckbox(Checkbox
        target);
    protected abstract CheckboxMenuItemPeer
        createCheckboxMenuItem(CheckboxMenuItem target);
    protected abstract ChoicePeer createChoice(Choice target);
        protected java.awt.peer.LightweightPeer
        createComponent(Component target)
    protected abstract DialogPeer createDialog(Dialog target);
    protected abstract FileDialogPeer
        createFileDialog(FileDialog target);
    protected abstract FramePeer createFrame(Frame target);
    public abstract Image createImage(ImageProducer producer);
    public Image createImage(byte[] imagedata)
    public abstract Image createImage(byte[] imagedata, int
```

(continued)

(continued)

```
        imageoffset, int imagelength);
protected abstract LabelPeer createLabel(Label target);
protected abstract ListPeer createList(List target);
protected abstract MenuPeer createMenu(Menu target);
protected abstract MenuBarPeer createMenuBar(MenuBar tar
    get);
protected abstract MenuItemPeer createMenuItem(MenuItem
    target);
protected abstract PanelPeer createPanel(Panel target);
protected abstract PopupMenuPeer createPopupMenu(PopupMenu
    target);
protected abstract ScrollbarPeer createScrollbar(Scrollbar
    target);
protected abstract ScrollPanePeer createScrollPane(ScrollPane
    target);
protected abstract TextAreaPeer createTextArea(TextArea
    target);
protected abstract TextFieldPeer createTextField(TextField
    target);
protected abstract WindowPeer createWindow(Window target);
public abstract ColorModel getColorModel();
public static synchronized Toolkit getDefaultToolkit()
public abstract String[] getFontList();
public abstract FontMetrics getFontMetrics(Font font);
protected abstract FontPeer getFontPeer(String name, int
    style);
public abstract Image getImage(String filename);
public abstract Image getImage(URL url);
public int getMenuShortcutKeyMask()
protected static Container getNativeContainer(Component c)
public abstract PrintJob getPrintJob(Frame frame, String
    jobtitle, Properties props);
public static String getProperty(String key, String
    defaultValue)
public final EventQueue getSystemEventQueue()
public abstract int getScreenResolution();
public abstract Dimension getScreenSize();
public abstract Clipboard getSystemClipboard();
protected void loadSystemColors(int[] systemColors)
public abstract boolean prepareImage(Image image, int width,
    int height, ImageObserver observer);
static
public abstract void sync();
```

java.awt.Window

Window is the superclass of Frame and Dialog. You can't create
an instance of Window unless you are in the AWT package. You use
Window to factor out commonality between Frame and Dialog.

If you want to create a standard window with a title bar, use Frame
(see "java.awt.Frame" in this part).

```
public class Window extends Container
    String warningString;
    public void addNotify()
    public synchronized void addWindowListener(WindowListener l)
    void dispatchEvent(AWTEvent e)
    public void dispose()
```

```
boolean eventEnabled(AWTEvent e)
public Component getFocusOwner()
public Locale getLocale()
public Toolkit getToolkit()
public final String getWarningString()
void nextFocus(Component base)
public synchronized void removeWindowListener(WindowListener l)
public void pack()
public boolean postEvent(Event e)
void postProcessKeyEvent(KeyEvent e)
void setFocusOwner(Component c)
public void show()
public void toBack()
public void toFront()
void transferFocus(Component base)
Window()
public Window(Frame parent)
```

The java.awt.datatransfer Package

The classes in the java.awtdatatransfer package provide a standard mechanism to transfer data within and between applications. In the 1.1 Version of the JDK, these classes support clipboard operations, such as cut, copy, and paste. Sun Microsystems plans to incorporate drag-and-drop capabilities in the next release of the JDK.

The class hierarchy for the java.awt.datatransfer package is shown in the following figure:

The clipboard model implies a level of persistence for the

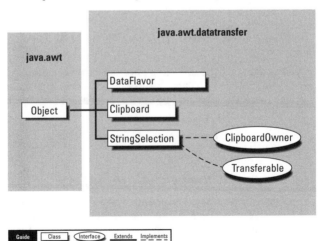

clipboard's contents. However, to avoid unnecessary performance penalties at cut and copy time, the data may not actually be transferred from the owner until it has been requested by a consumer (this is known as a *lazy* data model).

If the clipboard owner is destroyed, you may want to retrieve the data and store it in the clipboard to ensure its availability. The clipboard owner should not, however, make any assumptions about when the transfer will occur and should attempt to keep the data available until its lostOwnership() method is called. If the owner can't keep the data available indefinitely, then it should throw an IOException if the data is requested but is no longer available.

java.awt.datatransfer.Clipboard

This class provides a mechanism to transfer data using cut, copy, and paste operations. You find two basic methods in this class: setContents() and getContents() for reading from and writing to the clipboard, respectively.

```
public class Clipboard
    String name;
    protected ClipboardOwner owner;
    protected Transferable contents;
    public Clipboard(String name)
    public synchronized Transferable getContents(Object re
        questor)
    public String getName()
    public synchronized void setContents(Transferable contents,
        ClipboardOwner owner)
```

java.awt.datatransfer.ClipboardOwner

ClipboardOwner defines the method lostOwnership(). Any classes that provide data to a clipboard must define lostOwnership(). This method notifies the object that it no longer owns the contents of the clipboard.

```
public interface ClipboardOwner
    public void lostOwnership(Clipboard clipboard, Transferable
        contents);
```

java.awt.datatransfer.DataFlavor

You may want to take a moment to savor this class — it's got lots of flavor. So what does flavor have to do with Java programming? A *flavor* is simply the format that a transferable object uses to provide data. Think of DataFlavor as what you tell the ice-cream scooper at the ice-cream stand; if you ask for chocolate ice cream, then you expect to get chocolate, and not vanilla.

This class encapsulates all necessary information about a particular flavor so that flavor negotiation and transfer between applications can take place. For example, a data transfer operation (such as the clipboard) is a negotiation between the producer and the consumer on which flavor to transfer the data.

```
public class DataFlavor
    public static DataFlavor stringFlavor;
    public static DataFlavor plainTextFlavor;
    static final String serializedObjectMimeType;
    static Class ioInputStreamClass;
    int atom;
    public DataFlavor(Class representationClass, String
        humanPresentableName)
    public DataFlavor(String mimeType, String
        humanPresentableName)
    public boolean equals(DataFlavor dataFlavor)
    public String getHumanPresentableName()
    public String getMimeType()
    public Class getRepresentationClass()
    public boolean isMimeTypeEqual(String mimeType)
    public final boolean isMimeTypeEqual(DataFlavor dataFlavor)
    protected String normalizeMimeType(String mimeType)
    protected String normalizeMimeTypeParameter(String
        parameterName, String parameterValue)
    public void setHumanPresentableName(String
        humanPresentableName)
    static
```

java.awt.datatransfer.StringSelection

StringSelection isn't just for violin and cello players. In Java programming, StringSelection provides the capability to transfer a Java String in plain text format. Basically, StringSelection comes in handy when you want to cut and paste text.

```
public class StringSelection implements Transferable,
ClipboardOwner
    final static int STRING;
    final static int PLAIN_TEXT;
    DataFlavor flavors[];
    private String data;
    public synchronized Object getTransferData(DataFlavor
        flavor) throws UnsupportedFlavorException, IOException
    public synchronized DataFlavor[] getTransferDataFlavors()
    public boolean isDataFlavorSupported(DataFlavor flavor)
    public void lostOwnership(Clipboard clipboard, Transferable
        contents)
    public StringSelection(String data)
```

java.awt.datatransfer.Transferable

This somewhat repetitively named class defines the interface for classes that provide data for a transfer operation.

```
public interface Transferable
    public DataFlavor[] getTransferDataFlavors();
    public boolean isDataFlavorSupported(DataFlavor flavor);
    public Object getTransferData(DataFlavor flavor) throws
        UnsupportedFlavorException, IOException;
```

The java.awt.event Package

The classes and interfaces in the `java.awt.event` package support the delegation event model. You may find the delegation model more efficient than the conventional methods found in JDK 1.02.

The conventional methods are still supported and function as expected in JDK 1.1, but you shouldn't mix the conventional methods and the event delegation event model.

The following figures show the class hierarchy of the `java.awt.event` package:

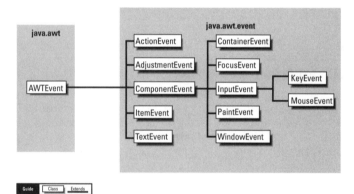

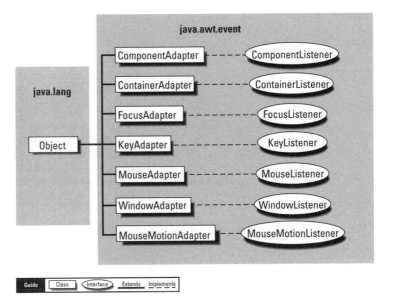

You find three types of objects in this package: events, adapters, and listeners. The events, such as `ActionEvent` or `MouseEvent`, contain information about events and are passed to event-handler methods. Adapters, such as `WindowAdapter` or `ComponentAdapter`, are abstract classes that you can extend in order to handle events. Listeners, such as `MouseMotionListener` or `ActionListener`, are interfaces that you can implement in order to handle events.

So what's the difference between adapters and listeners? Adapters are abstract classes, so you can extend only one of them. Listeners are interfaces, so you can implement as many as you like. If you can use as many listeners as you want to, why not always use listeners? Most listeners have more than one method specified, so you must fill in all of their methods, even if they don't do anything. Adapter methods by default don't do anything, so you only have to override the methods that interest you.

In the cases where only one method is specified, such as `ActionListener`, no corresponding adapter class exists. An abstract class for an interface with only one method provides no advatange, so it's not defined.

Getting a peek at inner classes and the delegation event model

JDK 1.1 introduces *inner classes* and the *delegation event model* to Java. Inner classes are simply classes that can be declared inside other classes. This feature has been used in other object-oriented languages with positive results, so Sun Microsystems decided to add it to Java. Interestingly, no modification to the virtual machine was necessary to support inner classes. The delegation event model was added to the AWT to improve performance in GUI applications. The traditional event model is still supported for backward compatibility but has been deprecated.

Inner classes have the same syntax as top level classes — the only difference is that inner classes are defined inside of another class. When a source file containing an inner class is compiled, a separate class file is generated for the inner class, just like a top-level class. The class file name is the name of the top-level class with the name of the inner class appended to it separated by a dollar sign ($).

For example, if you compile the source file in the following example, you get these class files: `Edit$FileCloseLis.class`, `Edit$FileNewLis.class`, `Edit$FileOpen.class`, `Edit$FileSaveAs.class`, `Edit$FileSave.class`, `Edit$WindowLis.class`, and `Edit.class`.

The inner classes have access to enclosing class instance and static variables.

The following example implements a simple text editor using the delegation event model and inner classes. The text editing happens in a text area for simplicity. A menu bar with a file menu is added. Each of the menu items has an `ActionListener` associated with it. The `ActionListener` is an inner class that implements the `ActionListener` interface and fills in the `actionPerformed()` method. The `ActionListener` is registered by using the `addActionListener()` method in the `MenuItem` class. When the user selects one of the menu items, the associated listener is called.

In the old event model, any and all action events would be passed to an `action()` method, and the programmer would have to figure out where the event came from to handle it. Needless to say, the old event model was not very efficient.

A `WindowListener` is also added to handle window-close events. File reading and writing uses the `Reader` and `Writer` subclasses instead of the `InputStream` and `OutputStream` subclasses. The `Reader` and `Writer` subclasses are preferred when working with character streams. `FileDialogs` for file loading and saving are used to present a more professional and user-friendly application. Other than that, the code is not much different than that of JDK 1.02.

```
import java.awt.*;
import java.awt.event.*;
```

```
import java.io.*;

public class Edit extends Frame {

String fileName;
Frame parentFrame;
TextArea textArea;
MenuBar menuBar;
Menu fileMenu;
MenuItem fmNew, fmOpen, fmClose, fmSave, fmSaveAs, fmQuit;

public Edit () {
    this ("Untitled");
}

public Edit (String fn) {
    super ("Edit - " + fn);
    fileName = fn;
    parentFrame = this;

    setLayout (new BorderLayout ());
    textArea = new TextArea ();
    add ("Center", textArea);
    addWindowListener (new WindowLis ());
    menuBar = new MenuBar ();

    fileMenu = new Menu ("File");
    fileMenu.add (fmNew = new MenuItem ("New"));
    fmNew.addActionListener (new FileNewLis ());

    fileMenu.add (fmOpen = new MenuItem ("Open"));
    fmOpen.addActionListener (new FileOpenLis ());

    fileMenu.add (fmClose = new MenuItem ("Close"));
    fmClose.addActionListener (new FileCloseLis ());

    fileMenu.add (fmSave = new MenuItem ("Save"));
    fmSave.addActionListener (new FileSaveLis ());

    fileMenu.add (fmSaveAs = new MenuItem ("Save as..."));
    fmSaveAs.addActionListener (new FileSaveAsLis ());

    fileMenu.addSeparator ();
    fileMenu.add (fmQuit = new MenuItem ("Quit"));
    fmQuit.addActionListener (new WindowLis ());
    menuBar.add (fileMenu);

    setMenuBar (menuBar);
    setSize (400, 300);
    show ();
}

class WindowLis extends WindowAdapter implements ActionListener {

    public void actionPerformed (ActionEvent e) {
        exitProgram ();
    }

    public void windowClosing (WindowEvent e) {
        exitProgram ();
    }
}
```

(continued)

(continued)

```java
class FileNewLis implements ActionListener {

    public void actionPerformed (ActionEvent e) {
        new Edit ();
    }
}

class FileOpenLis implements ActionListener {

    public void actionPerformed (ActionEvent e) {
        FileDialog fd = new FileDialog (parentFrame,
                "Open file...", FileDialog.LOAD);
        fd.show ();
        String fName = fd.getFile ();
        if (fName == null) return;
        Edit ed = new Edit (fName);
        ed.readFile ();
    }
}

class FileCloseLis implements ActionListener {

    public void actionPerformed (ActionEvent e) {
        if (fileName.equals ("Untitled")) {
                String fName = getFileName ();
                if (fName == null) return;
                fileName = fName;
                writeFile ();
        }
        parentFrame.dispose ();
    }
}

class FileSaveLis implements ActionListener {

    public void actionPerformed (ActionEvent e) {
        if (fileName.equals ("Untitled")) {
                String fName = getFileName ();
                if (fName == null) return;
                fileName = fName;
        }
        writeFile ();
        setTitle (fileName);
    }
}

class FileSaveAsLis implements ActionListener {

    public void actionPerformed (ActionEvent e) {
        String fName = getFileName ();
        if (fName == null) return;
        fileName = fName;
        writeFile ();
        setTitle (fileName);
    }
}

String getFileName () {
    FileDialog fd = new FileDialog (parentFrame,
        "Save file...", FileDialog.SAVE);
    fd.show ();
    return fd.getFile ();
```

```
        }
    void exitProgram () {
        System.exit (0);
    }

    void readFile () {
        try {
            BufferedReader br = new BufferedReader (
                    new FileReader (fileName));
            String line;
            line = br.readLine ();
            while (line != null) {
                    textArea.append (line + "\n");
                    line = br.readLine ();
            }
            br.close ();
        } catch (IOException e) {
            System.out.println (e);
        }
    }

    void writeFile () {
        try {
            PrintWriter ps = new PrintWriter (
                    new FileWriter (fileName));
            ps.print (textArea.getText ());
            ps.close ();
        } catch (IOException e) {
            System.out.println (e);
        }
    }

    public static void main (String args[]) {
        if (args.length == 0) new Edit ();
        else {
            for (int i=0; i<args.length; i+=1) {
                    Edit ed = new Edit (args[i]);
                    ed.readFile ();
            }
        }
    }
}
```

The following figure shows you the running application:

java.awt.event.ActionEvent

When an action occurs, an `ActionListener` receives an instance of this object. Actions can be button presses, menu item selections, return key strikes in a text field, and so on.

```
public class ActionEvent extends AWTEvent
    public static final int SHIFT_MASK;
    public static final int CTRL_MASK;
    public static final int META_MASK;
    public static final int ALT_MASK;
    public static final int ACTION_FIRST;
    public static final int ACTION_LAST;
    public static final int ACTION_PERFORMED;
    String actionCommand;
    int modifiers;
    public ActionEvent(Object source, int id, String command)
    public ActionEvent(Object source, int id, String command,
        int modifiers)
    public String getActionCommand()
    public int getModifiers()
    public String paramString()
```

java.awt.event.ActionListener

When you create a class to handle an action event, you should implement this interface and fill in the `actionPerformed` method. The result: You get an instance of `ActionListener` that describes the event.

```
public interface ActionListener extends EventListener
    public void actionPerformed(ActionEvent e);
```

java.awt.event.AdjustmentEvent

Use this class with adjustable components, such as scroll bars. Objects implementing the `AdjustmentListener` receive an instance of this class.

```
public class AdjustmentEvent extends AWTEvent
    public static final int ADJUSTMENT_FIRST;
    public static final int ADJUSTMENT_LAST;
    public static final int ADJUSTMENT_VALUE_CHANGED;
    public static final int UNIT_INCREMENT;
    public static final int UNIT_DECREMENT;
    public static final int BLOCK_DECREMENT;
    public static final int BLOCK_INCREMENT;
    public static final int TRACK;
    Adjustable adjustable;
    int value;
    int adjustmentType;
    public AdjustmentEvent(Adjustable source, int id, int type,
        int value)
    public Adjustable getAdjustable()
    public int getAdjustmentType()
    public int getValue()
    public String paramString()
```

java.awt.event.AdjustmentListener

If you want to handle adjustment events, such as scroll bar events, create a class that implements this interface and fill in the `adjustmentValueChanged` method. Your object receives an instance of `AdjustmentEvent` when an adjustment occurs. Note that no corresponding adapter class exists.

```
public interface AdjustmentListener extends EventListener
    public void adjustmentValueChanged(AdjustmentEvent e);
```

java.awt.event.ComponentAdapter

If you want to catch some general component events, extend this class and override the methods that interest you. Each of your methods receives an instance of `ComponentEvent` describing the event.

```
public abstract class ComponentAdapter implements
ComponentListener
    public void componentHidden(ComponentEvent e)
    public void componentMoved(ComponentEvent e)
    public void componentResized(ComponentEvent e)
    public void componentShown(ComponentEvent e)
```

java.awt.event.ComponentEvent

When a component event occurs (such as move, resize, show, and hide), an instance of this class goes to all `ComponentListeners` and `ComponentAdapters`.

```
public class ComponentEvent extends AWTEvent
    public static final int COMPONENT_FIRST;
    public static final int COMPONENT_LAST;
    public static final int COMPONENT_MOVED;
    public static final int COMPONENT_RESIZED;
    public static final int COMPONENT_SHOWN;
    public static final int COMPONENT_HIDDEN;
    public ComponentEvent(Component source, int id)
    public Component getComponent()
    public String paramString()
```

java.awt.event.ComponentListener

If you want to catch some general component events, such as resize and move, implement this interface and fill in the methods. Your class receives an instance of `ComponentEvent` when one of the component events occurs.

You have to fill in all of the methods in this interface, even if you don't do anything with them.

```
public interface ComponentListener extends EventListener
    public void componentResized(ComponentEvent e);
    public void componentMoved(ComponentEvent e);
    public void componentShown(ComponentEvent e);
    public void componentHidden(ComponentEvent e);
```

java.awt.event.ContainerAdapter

ContainerAdapter resembles ComponentAdapter, but ContainerAdapter works on containers, such as Panel or Frame. If you want to handle container events, extend this class and override the methods that interest you. Each of your methods receives an instance of ContainerEvent describing the event that occurred.

```
public abstract class ContainerAdapter implements
ContainerListener
    public void componentAdded(ContainerEvent e)
    public void componentRemoved(ContainerEvent e)
```

java.awt.event.ContainerEvent

An instance of this class is given to all ContainerListeners and ContainerAdapters when a Component is added or removed from a Container.

```
public class ContainerEvent extends ComponentEvent
    public static final int CONTAINER_FIRST;
    public static final int CONTAINER_LAST;
    public static final int COMPONENT_ADDED;
    public static final int COMPONENT_REMOVED;
    Component child;
    public ContainerEvent(Component source, int id, Component
        child)
    public Component getChild()
    public Container getContainer()
    public String paramString()
```

java.awt.event.ContainerListener

If you want to know when a Component was added or removed from a Container, implement this interface and fill in the methods. Each of your methods receives an instance of ContainerEvent describing the event that occurred.

```
public interface ContainerListener extends EventListener
    public void componentAdded(ContainerEvent e);
    public void componentRemoved(ContainerEvent e);
```

java.awt.event.FocusAdapter

FocusAdapter catches Component focus events. If you want to catch focus events, extend this class and override the methods

that interest you. Each of your methods receives an instance of
FocusEvent describing the event that occurred.

```
public abstract class FocusAdapter implements FocusListener
    public void focusGained(FocusEvent e)
    public void focusLost(FocusEvent e)
```

java.awt.event.FocusEvent

FocusAdapters and FocusListeners receive an instance of
this class when a component gains or loses focus.

```
public class FocusEvent extends ComponentEvent
    public static final int FOCUS_FIRST;
    public static final int FOCUS_LAST;
    public static final int FOCUS_GAINED;
    public static final int FOCUS_LOST;
    boolean temporary;
    public FocusEvent(Component source, int id, boolean
        temporary)
    public FocusEvent(Component source, int id)
    public boolean isTemporary()
    public String paramString()
```

java.awt.event.FocusListener

If you want to be notified when a component gains or loses focus,
implement this interface and fill in its methods. Each of your
methods receives an instance of FocusEvent describing the event
that occurred.

```
public interface FocusListener extends EventListener
    public void focusGained(FocusEvent e);
    public void focusLost(FocusEvent e);
```

java.awt.event.InputEvent

InputEvent is the superclass of other event classes, such as
KeyEvent and MouseEvent. The InputEvent class factors out
key modifiers, such as shift and control. You probably won't use
this class directly, but you may want to use its methods to find out
if the user was holding down the shift key when he or she dragged
the mouse, for example.

```
public abstract class InputEvent extends ComponentEvent
    public static final int SHIFT_MASK;
    public static final int CTRL_MASK;
    public static final int META_MASK;
    public static final int ALT_MASK;
    public static final int BUTTON1_MASK;
    public static final int BUTTON2_MASK;
    public static final int BUTTON3_MASK;
    long when;
    int modifiers;
```

(continued)

(continued)

```
public void consume()
public int getModifiers()
public long getWhen()
InputEvent(Component source, int id, long when, int
    modifiers)
public boolean isAltDown()
public boolean isConsumed()
public boolean isControlDown()
public boolean isMetaDown()
public boolean isShiftDown()
```

java.awt.event.ItemEvent

When you use ItemEvent in your code, an instance of
ItemEvent is passed to ItemListeners when a state change
occurs in a Component. ItemEvent is supported by components
that maintain state; a check box is an example of a Component
that maintains a state (on or off).

```
public class ItemEvent extends AWTEvent
    public static final int ITEM_FIRST;
    public static final int ITEM_LAST;
    public static final int ITEM_STATE_CHANGED;
    public static final int SELECTED;
    public static final int DESELECTED;
    Object item;
    int stateChange;
    public Object getItem()
    public ItemSelectable getItemSelectable()
    public int getStateChange()
    public ItemEvent(ItemSelectable source, int id, Object item,
        int stateChange)
    public String paramString()
```

java.awt.event.ItemListener

If you want to catch state change events, implement this interface
and fill in the method. Your class receives an instance of
ItemEvent when a state change occurs. (A state change event
occurs when a user clicks on a check box.) Note that there is no
corresponding adapter for this interface.

```
public interface ItemListener extends EventListener
    void itemStateChanged(ItemEvent e);
```

java.awt.event.KeyAdapter

KeyAdapter catches key events. If you want to handle key events,
extend this class and override the methods that interest you. Each
of the methods receives a KeyEvent object when a key event
occurs.

```
public abstract class KeyAdapter implements KeyListener
    public void keyPressed(KeyEvent e)
    public void keyReleased(KeyEvent e)
    public void keyTyped(KeyEvent e)
```

java.awt.event.KeyEvent

KeyEvent tells you everything you ever wanted to know about a key event. It can even tell you things that you don't want to know. KeyAdapters and KeyListeners receive an instance of KeyEvent when a key event occurs.

```
public class KeyEvent extends InputEvent
    public static final int KEY_FIRST;
    public static final int KEY_LAST;
    public static final int KEY_TYPED;
    public static final int KEY_PRESSED;
    public static final int KEY_RELEASED;
    public static final int VK_ENTER;
    public static final int VK_BACK_SPACE;
    public static final int VK_TAB;
    public static final int VK_CANCEL;
    public static final int VK_CLEAR;
    public static final int VK_SHIFT;
    public static final int VK_CONTROL;
    public static final int VK_ALT;
    public static final int VK_PAUSE;
    public static final int VK_CAPS_LOCK;
    public static final int VK_ESCAPE;
    public static final int VK_SPACE;
    public static final int VK_PAGE_UP;
    public static final int VK_PAGE_DOWN;
    public static final int VK_END;
    public static final int VK_HOME;
    public static final int VK_LEFT;
    public static final int VK_UP;
    public static final int VK_RIGHT;
    public static final int VK_DOWN;
    public static final int VK_COMMA;
    public static final int VK_PERIOD;
    public static final int VK_SLASH;
    public static final int VK_0;
    public static final int VK_1;
    public static final int VK_2;
    public static final int VK_3;
    public static final int VK_4;
    public static final int VK_5;
    public static final int VK_6;
    public static final int VK_7;
    public static final int VK_8;
    public static final int VK_9;
    public static final int VK_SEMICOLON;
    public static final int VK_EQUALS;
    public static final int VK_A;
    public static final int VK_B;
    public static final int VK_C;
    public static final int VK_D;
    public static final int VK_E;
    public static final int VK_F;
```

(continued)

(continued)

```
public static final int VK_G;
public static final int VK_H;
public static final int VK_I;
public static final int VK_J;
public static final int VK_K;
public static final int VK_L;
public static final int VK_M;
public static final int VK_N;
public static final int VK_O;
public static final int VK_P;
public static final int VK_Q;
public static final int VK_R;
public static final int VK_S;
public static final int VK_T;
public static final int VK_U;
public static final int VK_V;
public static final int VK_W;
public static final int VK_X;
public static final int VK_Y;
public static final int VK_Z;
public static final int VK_OPEN_BRACKET;
public static final int VK_BACK_SLASH;
public static final int VK_CLOSE_BRACKET;
public static final int VK_NUMPAD0;
public static final int VK_NUMPAD1;
public static final int VK_NUMPAD2;
public static final int VK_NUMPAD3;
public static final int VK_NUMPAD4;
public static final int VK_NUMPAD5;
public static final int VK_NUMPAD6;
public static final int VK_NUMPAD7;
public static final int VK_NUMPAD8;
public static final int VK_NUMPAD9;
public static final int VK_MULTIPLY;
public static final int VK_ADD;
public static final int VK_SEPARATER;
public static final int VK_SUBTRACT;
public static final int VK_DECIMAL;
public static final int VK_DIVIDE;
public static final int VK_F1;
public static final int VK_F2;
public static final int VK_F3;
public static final int VK_F4;
public static final int VK_F5;
public static final int VK_F6;
public static final int VK_F7;
public static final int VK_F8;
public static final int VK_F9;
public static final int VK_F10;
public static final int VK_F11;
public static final int VK_F12;
public static final int VK_DELETE;
public static final int VK_NUM_LOCK;
public static final int VK_SCROLL_LOCK;
public static final int VK_PRINTSCREEN;
public static final int VK_INSERT;
public static final int VK_HELP;
public static final int VK_META;
public static final int VK_BACK_QUOTE;
public static final int VK_QUOTE;
public static final int VK_UNDEFINED;
public static final char CHAR_UNDEFINED;
```

```
int keyCode;
char keyChar;
public char getKeyChar()
public int getKeyCode()
public static String getKeyModifiersText(int modifiers)
public static String getKeyText(int keyCode)
public boolean isActionKey()
public KeyEvent(Component source, int id, long when, int
    modifiers, int keyCode, char keyChar)
public KeyEvent(Component source, int id, long when, int
    modifiers, int keyCode)
public String paramString()
public void setKeyChar(char keyChar)
public void setKeyCode(int keyCode)
public void setModifiers(int modifiers)
```

java.awt.event.KeyListener

KeyListener comes in handy when you want to handle key
events. Just implement this interface and fill in the methods. Each
of the methods receives an instance of a KeyEvent object when a
key event occurs.

```
public interface KeyListener extends EventListener

    public void keyTyped(KeyEvent e);
    public void keyPressed(KeyEvent e);
    public void keyReleased(KeyEvent e);
```

java.awt.event.MouseAdapter

Think of MouseAdapter as the hunting cat of the
java.awt.event package: MouseAdapter catches mouse
events. To handle mouse events, extend this class and override
the methods that interest you. Each of these methods receives an
instance of MouseEvent when a mouse event occurs.

```
public abstract class MouseAdapter implements MouseListener

    public void mouseClicked(MouseEvent e)
    public void mouseEntered(MouseEvent e)
    public void mouseExited(MouseEvent e)
    public void mousePressed(MouseEvent e)
    public void mouseReleased(MouseEvent e)
```

java.awt.event.MouseEvent

This class contains all kinds of good information about a mouse
event, including a count of mouse clicks so that double and
multiple mouse clicks can be handled easily.

You can use this class to check for multiple mouse clicks to
perform some interesting tasks. For example, if the user clicks five
times, you can make the program display a "Stop Pressing My
Button" dialog box.

```
public class MouseEvent extends InputEvent
    public static final int MOUSE_FIRST;
    public static final int MOUSE_LAST;
    public static final int MOUSE_CLICKED;
    public static final int MOUSE_PRESSED;
    public static final int MOUSE_RELEASED;
    public static final int MOUSE_MOVED;
    public static final int MOUSE_ENTERED;
    public static final int MOUSE_EXITED;
    public static final int MOUSE_DRAGGED;
    int x;
    int y;
    int clickCount;
    boolean popupTrigger;
    public int getClickCount()
    public Point getPoint()
    public int getX()
    public int getY()
    public boolean isPopupTrigger()
    public MouseEvent(Component source, int id, long when, int
        modifiers, int x, int y, int clickCount, boolean
        popupTrigger)
    public String paramString()
    public synchronized void translatePoint(int x, int y)
```

java.awt.event.MouseListener

MouseListener helps you handle mouse events. If you implement this interface and fill in the methods, each of these methods
receives an instance of MouseEvent when a mouse event occurs.

```
public interface MouseListener extends EventListener
    public void mouseClicked(MouseEvent e);
    public void mousePressed(MouseEvent e);
    public void mouseReleased(MouseEvent e);
    public void mouseEntered(MouseEvent e);
    public void mouseExited(MouseEvent e);
```

java.awt.event.MouseMotionAdapter

This adapter catches mouse moves and drags. If you want to
handle these events, extend this class and override the methods
that interest you. Each of the methods receives an instance of
MouseEvent, which describes the event in detail.

```
public abstract class MouseMotionAdapter implements
MouseMotionListener
    public void mouseDragged(MouseEvent e)
    public void mouseMoved(MouseEvent e)
```

java.awt.event.MouseMotionListener

If you want to handle mouse drag and move events, implement
this interface and fill in the methods. Each of your methods
receives an instance of MouseEvent, which describes the event in
detail.

```
public interface MouseMotionListener extends EventListener
    public void mouseDragged(MouseEvent e);
    public void mouseMoved(MouseEvent e);
```

java.awt.event.PaintEvent

PaintEvent contains information about paint events, the most important being the destination Graphics object g.

```
public class PaintEvent extends ComponentEvent
    public static final int PAINT_FIRST;
    public static final int PAINT_LAST;
    public static final int PAINT;
    public static final int UPDATE;
    Graphics g;
    public Graphics getGraphics()
    public PaintEvent(Component source, int id, Graphics g)
    public String paramString()
```

java.awt.event.TextEvent

This class contains information about text component events. TextEvent is delivered to TextListeners when a text event occurs, such as a key strike in a text field.

```
public class TextEvent extends AWTEvent
    public static final int TEXT_FIRST;
    public static final int TEXT_LAST;
    public static final int TEXT_VALUE_CHANGED;
    public String paramString()
    public TextEvent(Object source, int id)
```

java.awt.event.TextListener

If you want to find out if something in a TextComponent has changed, implement this interface and fill in the method. Your method receives an instance of TextEvent when a text event occurs.

```
public interface TextListener extends EventListener
    public void textValueChanged(TextEvent e);
```

java.awt.event.WindowAdapter

The class catches window events, such as activate or iconify. If you want to handle events such as these, extend this class and override the methods that interest you. Each of your methods receives an instance of WindowEvent, which contains detailed information about the event.

When you create a Java application, you must create an event handler to handle the window closing, window destroy event, and exit from the application. If you don't create an event handler for these events, the application won't die when the user tries to close the window. You don't want your program to be a pest, do you?

```
public abstract class WindowAdapter implements WindowListener
    public void windowActivated(WindowEvent e)
    public void windowClosed(WindowEvent e)
    public void windowClosing(WindowEvent e)
    public void windowDeactivated(WindowEvent e)
    public void windowDeiconified(WindowEvent e)
    public void windowIconified(WindowEvent e)
    public void windowOpened(WindowEvent e)
```

java.awt.event.WindowEvent

WindowEvent provides useful information to WindowAdapters and WindowListeners when a window event occurs.

```
public class WindowEvent extends ComponentEvent
    public static final int WINDOW_FIRST;
    public static final int WINDOW_LAST;
    public static final int WINDOW_OPENED;
    public static final int WINDOW_CLOSING;
    public static final int WINDOW_CLOSED;
    public static final int WINDOW_ICONIFIED;
    public static final int WINDOW_DEICONIFIED;
    public static final int WINDOW_ACTIVATED;
    public static final int WINDOW_DEACTIVATED;
    public Window getWindow()
    public String paramString()
    public WindowEvent(Window source, int id)
```

java.awt.event.WindowListener

To handle window events, such as close or iconify, implement this interface and fill in all of the methods. Each of your methods receives an instance of WindowEvent, which contains detailed information about the event.

```
public interface WindowListener extends EventListener
    public void windowOpened(WindowEvent e);
    public void windowClosing(WindowEvent e);
    public void windowClosed(WindowEvent e);
    public void windowIconified(WindowEvent e);
    public void windowDeiconified(WindowEvent e);
    public void windowActivated(WindowEvent e);
    public void windowDeactivated(WindowEvent e);
```

The java.awt.image Package

The java.awt.image package contains several classes for image handling and processing. If all you want to do is load images and display them, don't worry about this package. The package is used by the rest of `awt` and `applet`, but it can be transparent (pardon the pun) to you.

We know you've been dying to get a peek at the `java.awt.image` package class hierarchy, so without further ado, we present it to you in the following figure:

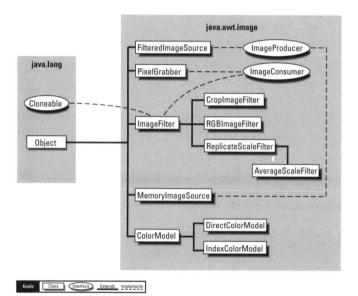

Slow network connections complicate the handling of images. The designers at Sun Microsystems created producers and consumers so that images download asynchronously. That means that you don't have to wait for your applet to continue just because it contains lots of images (such as the infamous Tumbling Duke).

This brings us to the subject of *image producers, observers,* and *consumers.* An image producer delivers an image; a consumer receives an image; and an observer watches the producers and consumers perform.

The details of these classes can get pretty gory, so study the classes closely if you plan to use them.

java.awt.image.AreaAveragingScaleFilter

`AreaAveragingScaleFilter` is an `ImageFilter` that you use in conjunction with `FilteredImageSource` to scale images. When you scale images up, pixels are replicated, and when you scale images down, pixels are averaged.

This class is very similar to `ReplicateScaleFilter`, except that `AreaAveragingScaleFilter` gets the pixels in order so that the scaling looks better.

```
public class AreaAveragingScaleFilter extends ReplicateScaleFilter
    ColorModel model, Object pixels, int off, int scansize)
    public AverageScaleFilter(int width, int height)
    private int[] calcRow()
    private void makeAccumBuffers()
    public void setHints(int hints)
    public void setPixels(int x, int y, int w, int h, ColorModel
        model, byte pixels[], int off, int scansize)
    public void setPixels(int x, int y, int w, int h, ColorModel
        model, int pixels[], int off, int scansize)
```

java.awt.image.ColorModel

This class defines a color model. `ColorModel` is abstract, so you can't create an instance of it directly. Other classes in this package use `ColorModel`.

```
public abstract class ColorModel
    protected int pixel_bits;
    public abstract int getRed(int pixel);
    public abstract int getGreen(int pixel);
    public abstract int getBlue(int pixel);
    public abstract int getAlpha(int pixel);
    public ColorModel(int bits)
    public void finalize()
    public int getPixelSize()
    public int getRGB(int pixel)
    public static ColorModel getRGBdefault()
```

java.awt.image.CropImageFilter

`CropImageFilter` is an image filter that crops an image to a particular size. You can apply this filter if you want to get a subset of an image.

```
public class CropImageFilter extends ImageFilter
    int cropX;
    int cropY;
    int cropW;
    int cropH;
    public CropImageFilter(int x, int y, int w, int h)
    public void setDimensions(int w, int h)
    public void setPixels(int x, int y, int w, int h, ColorModel
        model, byte pixels[], int off, int scansize)
    public void setPixels(int x, int y, int w, int h, ColorModel
        model, int pixels[], int off, int scansize)
    public void setProperties(Hashtable props)
```

java.awt.image.DirectColorModel

This color model maps red, green, blue, and alpha planes directly.

```
public class DirectColorModel extends ColorModel
    public DirectColorModel(int bits, int rmask, int gmask, int
        bmask)
    public DirectColorModel(int bits, int rmask, int gmask, int
        bmask, int amask)
    final public int getAlpha(int pixel)
    final public int getAlphaMask()
    final public int getBlue(int pixel)
    final public int getBlueMask()
    final public int getGreen(int pixel)
    final public int getGreenMask()
    final public int getRed(int pixel)
    final public int getRedMask()
    final public int getRGB(int pixel)
```

java.awt.image.FilteredImageSource

Use this class when you want to filter an image before it is used.
You may want to adjust some of the colors, for example.
FilteredImageSource works with an image producer and an
image filter.

```
public class FilteredImageSource implements ImageProducer
    ImageProducer src;
    ImageFilter filter;
    public synchronized void addConsumer(ImageConsumer ic)
    public FilteredImageSource(ImageProducer orig, ImageFilter
        imgf)
    public synchronized boolean isConsumer(ImageConsumer ic)
    public synchronized void removeConsumer(ImageConsumer ic)
    public void requestTopDownLeftRightResend(ImageConsumer ic)
    public void startProduction(ImageConsumer ic)
```

java.awt.image.ImageConsumer

This interface describes the methods required by an image
consumer.

```
public interface ImageConsumer
    void setDimensions(int width, int height);
    void setProperties(Hashtable props);
    void setColorModel(ColorModel model);
    void setHints(int hintflags);
    int RANDOMPIXELORDER;
    int TOPDOWNLEFTRIGHT;
    int COMPLETESCANLINES;
    int SINGLEPASS;
    int SINGLEFRAME;
    void setPixels(int x, int y, int w, int h, ColorModel model,
        byte pixels[], int off, int scansize);
    void setPixels(int x, int y, int w, int h, ColorModel model,
        int pixels[], int off, int scansize);
    void imageComplete(int status);
```

(continued)

(continued)

```
int IMAGEERROR;
int SINGLEFRAMEDONE;
int STATICIMAGEDONE;
int IMAGEABORTED;
```

java.awt.image.ImageFilter

This class works with `FilteredImageSource` to filter an image before it is used. This is the superclass of all image filters; it doesn't do any filtering by itself. If you want to define your own image filter, extend this class and override the methods of interest.

```
public class ImageFilter implements ImageConsumer, Cloneable

    protected ImageConsumer consumer;
    public Object clone()
    public ImageFilter getFilterInstance(ImageConsumer ic)
    public void imageComplete(int status)
    public void resendTopDownLeftRight(ImageProducer ip)
    public void setColorModel(ColorModel model)
    public void setDimensions(int width, int height)
    public void setHints(int hints)
    public void setPixels(int x, int y, int w, int h, ColorModel
    model, byte pixels[], int off, int scansize)
    public void setPixels(int x, int y, int w, int h, ColorModel
    model, int pixels[], int off, int scansize)
    public void setProperties(Hashtable props)
```

java.awt.image.ImageObserver

This interface is used by classes that receive images and want to get information about image production.
`Graphics.drawImage()` uses this interface to determine if the image has been fully delivered.

```
public interface ImageObserver

    public boolean imageUpdate(Image img, int infoflags, int x,
    int y, int width, int height);
    public static final int WIDTH;
    public static final int HEIGHT;
    public static final int PROPERTIES;
    public static final int SOMEBITS;
    public static final int FRAMEBITS;
    public static final int ALLBITS;
    public static final int ERROR;
    public static final int ABORT;
```

java.awt.image.Producer

This abstract class defines an image producer. `Producer` must be extended by other classes to be useful.

```
public interface ImageProducer

    public void addConsumer(ImageConsumer ic);
    public boolean isConsumer(ImageConsumer ic);
```

```
public void removeConsumer(ImageConsumer ic);
public void startProduction(ImageConsumer ic);
public void requestTopDownLeftRightResend(ImageConsumer ic);
```

java.awt.image.IndexColorModel

Use this class to map colors with fixed arrays.

```
public class IndexColorModel extends ColorModel
    final public int getAlpha(int pixel)
    final public void getAlphas(byte a[])
    final public int getBlue(int pixel)
    final public void getBlues(byte b[])
    final public int getGreen(int pixel)
    final public void getGreens(byte g[])
    final public int getMapSize()
    final public int getRed(int pixel)
    final public void getReds(byte r[])
    final public int getRGB(int pixel)
    final public int getTransparentPixel()
    public IndexColorModel(int bits, int size, byte r[], byte
        g[], byte b[])
    public IndexColorModel(int bits, int size, byte r[], byte
        g[], byte b[], int trans)
    public IndexColorModel(int bits, int size, byte r[], byte
        g[], byte b[], byte a[])
    public IndexColorModel(int bits, int size, byte cmap[], int
        start, boolean hasalpha)
    public IndexColorModel(int bits, int size, byte cmap[], int
        start, boolean hasalpha, int trans)
```

java.awt.image.MemoryImageSource

This image producer can create an image from an array of pixels in memory. You can use this class to create your own images for animation or to build a class that can read images stored in a proprietary format.

```
public class MemoryImageSource implements ImageProducer
    int width;
    int height;
    ColorModel model;
    Object pixels;
    int pixeloffset;
    int pixelscan;
    Hashtable properties;
    Vector theConsumers;
    boolean animating;
    boolean fullbuffers;
    public synchronized void addConsumer(ImageConsumer ic)
    public synchronized boolean isConsumer(ImageConsumer ic)
    public MemoryImageSource(int w, int h, ColorModel cm, byte[]
        pix, int off, int scan)
    public MemoryImageSource(int w, int h, ColorModel cm, byte[]
        pix, int off, int scan, Hashtable props)
    public MemoryImageSource(int w, int h, ColorModel cm, int[]
        pix, int off, int scan)
```

(continued)

(continued)

```
public MemoryImageSource(int w, int h, ColorModel cm, int[]
    pix, int off, int scan, Hashtable props)
public MemoryImageSource(int w, int h, int pix[], int off,
    int scan)
public MemoryImageSource(int w, int h, int pix[], int off,
    int scan, Hashtable props)
public void newPixels()
public synchronized void newPixels(int x, int y, int w, int
    h)
public synchronized void newPixels(int x, int y, int w, int
    h, boolean framenotify)
public synchronized void newPixels(byte[] newpix, ColorModel
    newmodel, int offset, int scansize)
public synchronized void newPixels(int[] newpix, ColorModel
    newmodel, int offset, int scansize)
public synchronized void removeConsumer(ImageConsumer ic)
public void requestTopDownLeftRightResend(ImageConsumer ic)
public synchronized void setAnimated(boolean animated)
public synchronized void setFullBufferUpdates(boolean
    fullbuffers)
public void startProduction(ImageConsumer ic)
```

java.awt.image.PixelGrabber

Hold on to your pixels — here comes `PixelGrabber`! This
naughty little class does the opposite of `MemoryImageSource`.
`PixelGrabber` takes an `Image` object and produces an array of
pixel values.

```
public class PixelGrabber implements ImageConsumer
    ImageProducer producer;
    int dstX;
    int dstY;
    int dstW;
    int dstH;
    ColorModel imageModel;
    byte[] bytePixels;
    int[] intPixels;
    int dstOff;
    int dstScan;
    public synchronized void abortGrabbing()
    public synchronized ColorModel getColorModel()
    public synchronized int getHeight()
    public synchronized Object getPixels()
    public synchronized int getStatus()
    public synchronized int getWidth()
    public boolean grabPixels() throws InterruptedException
    public synchronized boolean grabPixels(long ms) throws
        InterruptedException
    public synchronized void imageComplete(int status)
    public PixelGrabber(Image img, int x, int y, int w, int h,
        int[] pix, int off, int scansize)
    public PixelGrabber(ImageProducer ip, int x, int y, int w,
        int h, int[] pix, int off, int scansize)
    public PixelGrabber(Image img, int x, int y, int w, int h,
        boolean forceRGB)
    public void setColorModel(ColorModel model)
    public void setDimensions(int width, int height)
    public void setHints(int hints)
    public void setPixels(int srcX, int srcY, int srcW, int
```

```
srcH, ColorModel model, byte pixels[], int srcOff, int
  srcScan)
public void setPixels(int srcX, int srcY, int srcW, int
  srcH, ColorModel model, int pixels[], int srcOff, int
  srcScan)
public void setProperties(Hashtable props)
public synchronized void startGrabbing()
public synchronized int status()
```

java.awt.image.RGBImageFilter

RGBImageFilter, an image filter, can modify pixel values using a method instead of a fixed array. If you want to filter an image using some arbitrary function, extend this class and override the filterRGB() method. Your method will be called for each pixel that is delivered from an ImageProducer.

```
public abstract class RGBImageFilter extends ImageFilter
    protected ColorModel origmodel;
    protected ColorModel newmodel;
    protected boolean canFilterIndexColorModel;
    public abstract int filterRGB(int x, int y, int rgb);
    public IndexColorModel filterIndexColorModel(IndexColorModel
      icm)
    public void filterRGBPixels(int x, int y, int w, int h, int
      pixels[], int off, int scansize)
    public void setColorModel(ColorModel model)
    public void setPixels(int x, int y, int w, int h, ColorModel
      model, byte pixels[], int off, int scansize)
    public void setPixels(int x, int y, int w, int h, ColorModel
      model, int pixels[], int off, int scansize)
    public void substituteColorModel(ColorModel oldcm,
      ColorModel newcm)
```

java.awt.image.ReplicateScaleFilter

ReplicateScaleFilter, an image filter, works in conjunction with FilteredImageSource to scale images. When you scale images up, pixels are replicated. When you scale images down, pixels are averaged.

```
public class ReplicateScaleFilter extends ImageFilter
    protected int srcWidth;
    protected int srcHeight;
    protected int destWidth;
    protected int destHeight;
    protected int srcrows[];
    protected int srccols[];
    protected Object outpixbuf;
    private void calculateMaps()
    public ReplicateScaleFilter(int width, int height)
    public void setDimensions(int w, int h)
    public void setPixels(int x, int y, int w, int h, ColorModel
      model, byte pixels[], int off, int scansize)
    public void setPixels(int x, int y, int w, int h, ColorModel
      model, int pixels[], int off, int scansize)
    public void setProperties(Hashtable props)
```

The java.io Package

What's a programming language without input/output functions? Not a very useful language, that's what! So here it is: the package that offers everything you ever wanted from an I/O library.

The java.io package looks really complicated, but it's not that bad. If you just want to read and write bytes, the java.io package offers a few simple classes to do just that. We don't mean to imply that the package only accomplishes simple functions: It also offers plenty of sophisticated classes.

Please allow us the privilege of showing you the unique and exciting hierarchy diagrams for the java.io package:

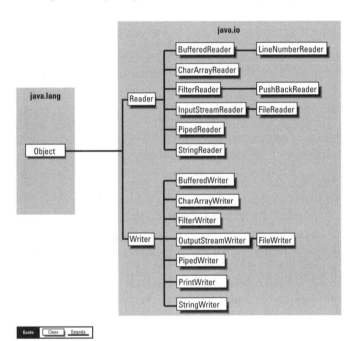

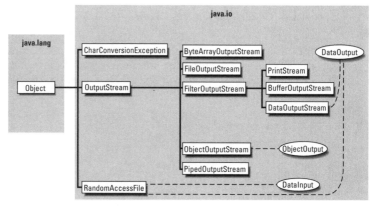

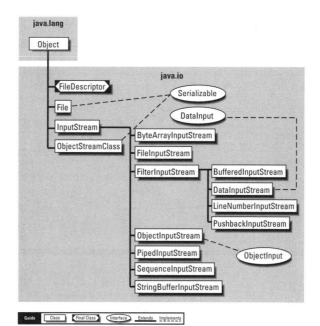

java.io.BufferedInputStream

InputStream is a non-buffered I/O stream. If you want buffered I/O, this is the class for you. It's a low-level class that just reads bytes and byte arrays. This stream lets you read in characters without causing a read every time. Take a look at the other classes if you want to add high level functionality.

```
public class BufferedInputStream extends FilterInputStream
    protected byte buf[];
    protected int count;
    protected int pos;
    protected int markpos;
    protected int marklimit;
    public synchronized int available() throws IOException
    public BufferedInputStream(InputStream in)
    public BufferedInputStream(InputStream in, int size)
    private void fill() throws IOException
    public synchronized void mark(int readlimit)
    public boolean markSupported()
    public synchronized int read() throws IOException
    public synchronized int read(byte b[], int off, int len)
        throws IOException
    public synchronized void reset() throws IOException
    public synchronized long skip(long n) throws IOException
```

java.io.BufferedOutputStream

BufferedOutputStream is just the opposite of BufferedInputStream. As the name suggests, it creates a buffered output stream. Like BufferedInputStream, BufferedOutputStream is a low-level class that just writes bytes and byte arrays. This stream lets you write characters to a stream without causing a write every time. The data is first written into a buffer. The data is only written into the actual stream when the buffer is full or when the stream is flushed.

```
public class BufferedOutputStream extends FilterOutputStream
    protected byte buf[];
    protected int count;
    public BufferedOutputStream(OutputStream out)
    public BufferedOutputStream(OutputStream out, int size)
    public synchronized void flush() throws IOException
    public synchronized void write(int b) throws IOException
    public synchronized void write(byte b[], int off, int len)
        throws IOException
```

java.io.BufferedReader

BufferedReader (which is similar to BufferedInputStream) works on character streams to provide efficient reading of characters, arrays, and lines. BufferedReader has some useful methods, such as readLine( ), which reads a line of text from a Reader stream.

```
public class BufferedReader extends Reader

    public BufferedReader(Reader in, int sz)
    public BufferedReader(Reader in)
    public void close() throws IOException
    public void mark(int readAheadLimit) throws IOException
    public boolean markSupported()
    public int read() throws IOException
    public int read(char cbuf[], int off, int len) throws
        IOException
    public String readLine() throws IOException
    public boolean ready() throws IOException
    public void reset() throws IOException
    public long skip(long n) throws IOException
```

java.io.BufferedWriter

BufferedWriter does just the opposite of BufferedReader; it
writes to character streams. BufferedWriter contains a
newLine() method, which writes a line terminator to a Writer
stream. The line terminator is platform dependent and works as
defined by the system property line.separator. Because not all
platforms use the newline character (\n) to terminate lines, calling
this method to terminate each output line is preferred to writing a
newline character directly.

```
public class BufferedWriter extends Writer

    public BufferedWriter(Writer out)
    public BufferedWriter(Writer out, int sz)
    public void close() throws IOException
    public void flush() throws IOException
    void flushBuffer() throws IOException
    public void newLine() throws IOException
    public void write(int c) throws IOException
    public void write(char cbuf[], int off, int len) throws
        IOException
    public void write(String s, int off, int len) throws
        IOException
```

java.io.ByteArrayInputStream

ByteArrayInputStream is a simple class for reading an array of
bytes from an InputStream. You can use the available()
method to determine how many bytes are available for reading.

```
public class ByteArrayInputStream extends InputStream

    protected byte buf[];
    protected int pos;
    protected int count;
    public synchronized int available()
    public ByteArrayInputStream(byte buf[])
    public ByteArrayInputStream(byte buf[], int offset, int
        length)
    public synchronized int read()
    public synchronized int read(byte b[], int off, int len)
    public synchronized void reset()
    public synchronized long skip(long n)
```

java.io.ByteArrayOutputStream

ByteArrayOutputStream writes an array of bytes to an OutputStream.

```
public class ByteArrayOutputStream extends OutputStream

    protected byte buf[];
    protected int count;
    public ByteArrayOutputStream()
    public ByteArrayOutputStream(int size)
    public synchronized void reset()
    public int size()
    public synchronized byte toByteArray()[]
    public String toString()
    public String toString(String enc) throws
        UnsupportedEncodingException
    public String toString(int hibyte)
    public synchronized void write(int b)
    public synchronized void write(byte b[], int off, int len)
    public synchronized void writeTo(OutputStream out) throws
        IOException
```

java.io.CharArrayReader

This class reads (Unicode) characters from a Reader stream. The ready() method tells you if the stream is ready for reading.

```
public class CharArrayReader extends Reader

    protected char buf[];
    protected int pos;
    protected int markedPos;
    protected int count;
    public CharArrayReader(char buf[])
    public CharArrayReader(char buf[], int offset, int length)
    public void close()
    public void mark(int readAheadLimit) throws IOException
    public boolean markSupported()
    public int read() throws IOException
    public int read(char b[], int off, int len) throws
        IOException
    public boolean ready() throws IOException
    public void reset() throws IOException
    public long skip(long n) throws IOException
```

java.io.CharArrayWriter

This class writes (Unicode) characters to a Writer stream.

The data is only written when the buffer is full or when the stream is flushed. Use the flush() method if you want to make sure data has been written to the stream.

```
public class CharArrayWriter extends Writer

    protected char buf[];
    protected int count;
    public CharArrayWriter()
    public CharArrayWriter(int initialSize)
    public void close()
```

```
public void flush()
public void reset()
public int size()
public char toCharArray()[]
public String toString()
public void write(int c)
public void write(char c[], int off, int len)
public void write(String str, int off, int len)
public void writeTo(Writer out) throws IOException
```

java.io.DataInput

Other classes in this package, such as `DataInputStream`, use this interface to describe an input stream.

```
public interface DataInput
    boolean readBoolean() throws IOException;
    byte readByte() throws IOException;
    char readChar() throws IOException;
    double readDouble() throws IOException;
    float readFloat() throws IOException;
    void readFully(byte b[]) throws IOException;
    void readFully(byte b[], int off, int len) throws
        IOException;
    int readInt() throws IOException;
    String readLine() throws IOException;
    long readLong() throws IOException;
    short readShort() throws IOException;
    int readUnsignedByte() throws IOException;
    int readUnsignedShort() throws IOException;
    String readUTF() throws IOException;
    int skipBytes(int n) throws IOException;
```

java.io.DataInputStream

`DataInputStream` is one of the most commonly used classes in the package. `DataInputStream` can read data from all platforms, and so you don't have to worry about reading "big-endian" data on a "little-endian" machine.

```
public class DataInputStream extends FilterInputStream implements
DataInput
    public DataInputStream(InputStream in)
    public final int read(byte b[]) throws IOException
    public final int read(byte b[], int off, int len) throws
        IOException
    public final boolean readBoolean() throws IOException
    public final byte readByte() throws IOException
    public final char readChar() throws IOException
    public final double readDouble() throws IOException
    public final float readFloat() throws IOException
    public final void readFully(byte b[]) throws IOException
    public final void readFully(byte b[], int off, int len)
        throws IOException
    public final int readInt() throws IOException
    public final String readLine() throws IOException
    public final long readLong() throws IOException
```

(continued)

(continued)
```
public final short readShort() throws IOException
public final int readUnsignedByte() throws IOException
public final int readUnsignedShort() throws IOException
public final String readUTF() throws IOException
public final static String readUTF(DataInput in) throws
    IOException
public final int skipBytes(int n) throws IOException
```

java.io.DataOutput

Other classes in this package, such as DataOutputStream, use
this interface to define a data output stream.

```
public interface DataOutput
    void write(int b) throws IOException;
    void write(byte b[]) throws IOException;
    void write(byte b[], int off, int len) throws IOException;
    void writeBoolean(boolean v) throws IOException;
    void writeByte(int v) throws IOException;
    void writeBytes(String s) throws IOException;
    void writeChar(int v) throws IOException;
    void writeChars(String s) throws IOException;
    void writeDouble(double v) throws IOException;
    void writeFloat(float v) throws IOException;
    void writeInt(int v) throws IOException;
    void writeLong(long v) throws IOException;
    void writeShort(int v) throws IOException;
    void writeUTF(String str) throws IOException;
```

java.io.DataOutputStream

DataOutputStream is the counterpart to DataInputStream.
This class writes data to all platforms, making the "endian-ness" of
machines not an issue.

```
public class DataOutputStream extends FilterOutputStream
implements DataOutput
    protected int written;
    public DataOutputStream(OutputStream out)
    public void flush() throws IOException
    public final int size()
    public synchronized void write(int b) throws IOException
    public synchronized void write(byte b[], int off, int len)
        throws IOException
    public final void writeBoolean(boolean v) throws IOException
    public final void writeByte(int v) throws IOException
    public final void writeBytes(String s) throws IOException
    public final void writeChar(int v) throws IOException
    public final void writeChars(String s) throws IOException
    public final void writeDouble(double v) throws IOException
    public final void writeFloat(float v) throws IOException
    public final void writeInt(int v) throws IOException
    public final void writeLong(long v) throws IOException
    public final void writeShort(int v) throws IOException
    public final void writeUTF(String str) throws IOException
```

java.io.Externalizable

Externalizable is an interface that specifies the methods a class may implement to read and write its contents to a stream. The methods readExternal and writeExternal must be filled in to perform the reading and writing.

```
public interface Externalizable extends java.io.Serializable
    void readExternal(ObjectInput in) throws IOException,
        ClassNotFoundException;
    void writeExternal(ObjectOutput out) throws IOException;
```

java.io.File

File collects information about files and directories.

File does not encapsulate a file pointer like the C structure with the same name.

```
public class File implements java.io.Serializable
    public static final String separator;
    public static final char separatorChar;
    public static final String pathSeparator;
    public static final char pathSeparatorChar;
    public boolean canRead()
    public boolean canWrite()
    public boolean delete()
    public boolean equals(Object obj)
    public boolean exists()
    public File(String path)
    public File(String path, String name)
    public File(File dir, String name)
    public String getAbsolutePath()
    public String getCanonicalPath() throws IOException
    public String getName()
    public String getParent()
    public String getPath()
    public int hashCode()
    public native boolean isAbsolute();
    public boolean isDirectory()
    public boolean isFile()
    public long lastModified()
    public long length()
    public String[] list()
    public String[] list(FilenameFilter filter)
    public boolean mkdir()
    public boolean mkdirs()
    public boolean renameTo(File dest)
    public String toString()
```

java.io.FileDescriptor

This class provides a system-dependent file descriptor. FileDescriptor offers a sync() method that you can call in order to sync with the underlying physical device.

This class does not have a public constructor. To obtain a FileDescriptor object, you can use the getFD() method from FileInputStream, FileOutputStream, or RandomAccessFile.

```
public final class FileDescriptor
    public static final FileDescriptor in;
    public static final FileDescriptor out;
    public static final FileDescriptor err;
    public native void sync() throws SyncFailedException;
    public native boolean valid();
```

java.io.FileInputStream

Use this class if you plan to open a file for reading. You can give FileInputStream a file name, a File object, or a FileDescriptor to specify the file. You can use this class to read data directly, but most programmers create another object (such as DataInputStream) and use its methods to read data.

```
public class FileInputStream extends InputStream
    public native int available() throws IOException;
    public native void close() throws IOException;
    public FileInputStream(String name) throws
        FileNotFoundException
    public FileInputStream(File file) throws
        FileNotFoundException
    public FileInputStream(FileDescriptor fdObj)
    protected void finalize() throws IOException
    public final FileDescriptor getFD() throws IOException
    public native int read() throws IOException;
    public int read(byte b[]) throws IOException
    public int read(byte b[], int off, int len) throws
        IOException
    public native long skip(long n) throws IOException;
```

java.io.FileNotFoundException

A number of classes in this package may throw this exception in the event of a non-existent file or directory. Don't be surprised if you see it from time to time.

```
public class FileNotFoundException extends IOException
    public FileNotFoundException()
    public FileNotFoundException(String s)
```

java.io.FileOutputStream

Use this class to open a file for writing. You can use the methods in this class directly, but most programmers create another object, such as PrintStream or DataOutputStream, and use the other object's methods for writing.

```
public class FileOutputStream extends OutputStream
    public native void close() throws IOException;
    public FileOutputStream(String name) throws IOException
    public FileOutputStream(String name, boolean append) throws
        IOException
    public FileOutputStream(File file) throws IOException
    public FileOutputStream(FileDescriptor fdObj)
    protected void finalize() throws IOException
    public final FileDescriptor getFD() throws IOException
    public native void write(int b) throws IOException;
    public void write(byte b[]) throws IOException
    public void write(byte b[], int off, int len) throws
        IOException
```

java.io.FileReader

FileReader reads Unicode characters from a file. You can't imagine how much fun this class has on a weeknight.

```
public class FileReader extends InputStreamReader
    public FileReader(String fileName) throws
        FileNotFoundException
    public FileReader(File file) throws FileNotFoundException
    public FileReader(FileDescriptor fd)
```

java.io.FileWriter

FileWriter writes Unicode characters to a file. When this class isn't writing Unicode to a file, it enjoys hiking, boating, and reading poetry.

```
public class FileWriter extends OutputStreamWriter
    public FileWriter(String fileName) throws IOException
    public FileWriter(String fileName, boolean append) throws
        IOException
    public FileWriter(File file) throws IOException
    public FileWriter(FileDescriptor fd)
```

java.io.FilenameFilter

We dare you to say FilenameFilter ten times, fast. You can use FilenameFilter together with the File.list() method or FileDialog to filter file names.

```
public interface FilenameFilter
    boolean accept(File dir, String name);
```

java.io.FilterInputStream

Several other classes in this package use FilterInputStream to chain several classes together for added functionality.

Remember: The class hierarchy diagram at the beginning of this section shows the relationship of this class to the other classes in the package.

```
public class FilterInputStream extends InputStream

    protected InputStream in;
    public int available() throws IOException
    public void close() throws IOException
    protected FilterInputStream(InputStream in)
    public synchronized void mark(int readlimit)
    public boolean markSupported()
    public int read() throws IOException
    public int read(byte b[]) throws IOException
    public int read(byte b[], int off, int len) throws
        IOException
    public synchronized void reset() throws IOException
    public long skip(long n) throws IOException
```

java.io.FilterOutputStream

Several other classes in this package use this class to chain
several classes together for added functionality. The best way to
visualize the relationship between classes is to draw a hierarchy
diagram. Lucky for you, we already put together a diagram for you.
Refer to the diagram at the beginning of this section for the
relationship of this class to others.

```
public class FilterOutputStream extends OutputStream

    protected OutputStream out;
    public void close() throws IOException
    public FilterOutputStream(OutputStream out)
    public void flush() throws IOException
    public void write(int b) throws IOException
    public void write(byte b[]) throws IOException
    public void write(byte b[], int off, int len) throws
        IOException
```

java.io.FilterReader

Several other classes in this package use this class to chain
several classes together for added functionality.

```
public abstract class FilterReader extends Reader

    protected Reader in;
    public void close() throws IOException
    protected FilterReader(Reader in)
    public void mark(int readAheadLimit) throws IOException
    public boolean markSupported()
    public int read() throws IOException
    public int read(char cbuf[], int off, int len) throws
        IOException
    public boolean ready() throws IOException
    public void reset() throws IOException
    public long skip(long n) throws IOException
```

java.io.FilterWriter

Several other classes in this package use this class to chain
several classes together for added functionality.

```
public abstract class FilterWriter extends Writer
    protected Writer out;
    public void close() throws IOException
    protected FilterWriter(Writer out)
    public void flush() throws IOException
    public void write(int c) throws IOException
    public void write(char cbuf[], int off, int len) throws
        IOException
    public void write(String str, int off, int len) throws
        IOException
```

java.io.InputStream

InputStream is the top of the "input" classes. This class is abstract, so you can't create an instance of InputStream directly — someone else gives it to you. It's more common to use other classes for input, such as DataInputStream.

```
public abstract class InputStream
    abstract public int available() throws IOException;
    public void close() throws IOException
    public synchronized void mark(int readlimit)
    public boolean markSupported()
    public abstract int read() throws IOException;
    public int read(byte b[]) throws IOException
    public int read(byte b[], int off, int len) throws
        IOException
    public synchronized void reset() throws IOException
    public long skip(long n) throws IOException
```

java.io.InputStreamReader

This class is the bridge between byte streams and character streams. It reads bytes and translates them into characters according to a specified character encoding. You can either specify the encoding or accept the platform's default encoding.

```
public class InputStreamReader extends Reader
    public void close() throws IOException
    public String getEncoding()
    public InputStreamReader(InputStream in)
    public InputStreamReader(InputStream in, String enc) throws
        UnsupportedEncodingException
    public int read() throws IOException
    public int read(char cbuf[], int off, int len) throws
        IOException
    public boolean ready() throws IOException
```

java.io.LineNumberInputStream

LineNumberInputStream may have one of the longest names in the whole package (21 letters). You can use this heftily named class to count lines from an InputStream, which comes in handy when you want to know how many lines you've read.

```
public class LineNumberInputStream extends FilterInputStream
    int pushBack;
    int lineNumber;
    int markLineNumber;
    public int available() throws IOException
    public int getLineNumber()
    public LineNumberInputStream(InputStream in)
    public void mark(int readlimit)
    public int read() throws IOException
    public int read(byte b[], int off, int len) throws
        IOException
    public void reset() throws IOException
    public void setLineNumber(int lineNumber)
    public long skip(long n) throws IOException
```

java.io.LineNumberReader

Counting lines from a Reader stream is easy when you use LineNumberReader. You'll never have to spend hours counting those tiny little lines again.

```
public class LineNumberReader extends BufferedReader
    public int getLineNumber()
    public LineNumberReader(Reader in)
    public LineNumberReader(Reader in, int sz)
    public void mark(int readAheadLimit) throws IOException
    public int read() throws IOException
    public int read(char cbuf[], int off, int len) throws
        IOException
    public String readLine() throws IOException
    public void reset() throws IOException
    public void setLineNumber(int lineNumber)
    public long skip(long n) throws IOException
```

java.io.ObjectInput

This interface works with ObjectInputStream.

```
public interface ObjectInput extends DataInput
    public int available() throws IOException;
    public void close() throws IOException;
    public int read() throws IOException;
    public int read(byte b[]) throws IOException;
    public int read(byte b[], int off, int len) throws
        IOException;
    public Object readObject() throws ClassNotFoundException,
        IOException;
    public long skip(long n) throws IOException;
```

java.io.ObjectInputStream

This class allows you to read an object that has been serialized using ObjectOutputStream.

```
public class ObjectInputStream extends InputStream
implements ObjectInput, ObjectStreamConstants
    ObjectStreamClass[] classdesc;
    Class[] classes;
    int spClass;
    public int available() throws IOException
    public void close() throws IOException
    public final void defaultReadObject() throws IOException,
        ClassNotFoundException, NotActiveException
    protected final boolean enableResolveObject(boolean enable)
        throws SecurityException
    public ObjectInputStream(InputStream in) throws IOException,
        StreamCorruptedException
    public int read() throws IOException
    public int read(byte[] data, int offset, int length) throws
        IOException
    public boolean readBoolean() throws IOException
    public byte readByte() throws IOException
    public char readChar() throws IOException
    public double readDouble() throws IOException
    public float readFloat() throws IOException
    public void readFully(byte[] data) throws IOException
    public void readFully(byte[] data, int offset, int size)
        throws IOException
    public int readInt() throws IOException
    public String readLine() throws IOException
    public long readLong() throws IOException
    public final Object readObject() throws
        OptionalDataException, ClassNotFoundException, IOException
    public short readShort() throws IOException
        protected void readStreamHeader() throws IOException,
        StreamCorruptedException
    public int readUnsignedByte() throws IOException
    public int readUnsignedShort() throws IOException
    public String readUTF() throws IOException
    public synchronized void
        registerValidation(ObjectInputValidation obj, int prio)
        throws NotActiveException,
        InvalidObjectExceptiregistervalidation
    protected Class resolveClass(ObjectStreamClass v) throws
        IOException, ClassNotFoundException
    protected Object resolveObject(Object obj) throws
        IOException
    public int skipBytes(int len) throws IOException
```

java.io.ObjectInputValidation

Another interface for you to use with object serialization (see "java.io.ObjectInputStream" in this part).

ObjectInputValidation defines a method for object validation.

```
public interface ObjectInputValidation
    public void validateObject() throws InvalidObjectException;
```

java.io.ObjectOutput

This interface works with `ObjectOutputStream`.

```
public interface ObjectOutput extends DataOutput
    public void close() throws IOException;
    public void flush() throws IOException;
    public void write(int b) throws IOException;
    public void write(byte b[]) throws IOException;
    public void write(byte b[], int off, int len) throws
        IOException;
    public void writeObject(Object obj) throws IOException;
```

java.io.ObjectOutputStream

You should use `ObjectOutputStream` with object serialization. This class does the opposite of `ObjectInputStream`.

```
public class ObjectOutputStream extends OutputStream implements
ObjectOutput, ObjectStreamConstants
    protected void annotateClass(Class cl) throws IOException
    public void close() throws IOException
    public final void defaultWriteObject() throws IOException
    protected void drain() throws IOException
    protected final boolean enableReplaceObject(boolean enable)
        throws SecurityException
    public void flush() throws IOException
    public ObjectOutputStream(OutputStream out) throws
        IOException
    protected Object replaceObject(Object obj) throws
        IOException
    public void reset() throws IOException
    public void write(int data) throws IOException
    public void write(byte b[]) throws IOException
    public void write(byte b[], int off, int len) throws
        IOException
    public void writeBoolean(boolean data) throws IOException
    public void writeByte(int data) throws IOException
    public void writeBytes(String data) throws IOException
    public void writeChar(int data) throws IOException
    public void writeChars(String data) throws IOException
    public void writeDouble(double data) throws IOException
    public void writeFloat(float data) throws IOException
    public void writeInt(int data) throws IOException
    public void writeLong(long data) throws IOException
    public final void writeObject(Object obj) throws IOException
    public void writeShort(int data) throws IOException
    protected void writeStreamHeader() throws IOException
    public void writeUTF(String data) throws IOException
```

java.io.ObjectStreamClass

`ObjectStreamClass` describes a class that can be or has been serialized to a stream.

```
public class ObjectStreamClass implements java.io.Serializable
    static private ObjectStreamClassEntry[] descriptorFor;
    public Class forClass()
    ObjectStreamField[] getFields()
```

```
public String getName()
public long getSerialVersionUID()
ObjectStreamClass getSuperclass()
boolean hasWriteReadMethods()
boolean isExternalizable()
ObjectStreamClass localClassDescriptor()
public static ObjectStreamClass lookup(Class cl)
ObjectStreamClass(String n, long s)
void read(ObjectInputStream s) throws IOException,
  ClassNotFoundException
void setClass(Class cl) throws InvalidClassException
void setSuperclass(ObjectStreamClass s)
static
public String toString()
boolean typeEquals(ObjectStreamClass other)
void write(ObjectOutputStream s) throws IOException
```

java.io.ObjectStreamConstants

ObjectStreamConstants describes constants used with object streams.

```
interface ObjectStreamConstants
    final static short STREAM_MAGIC;
    final static short STREAM_VERSION;
    final static byte TC_BASE;
    final static byte TC_NULL;
    final static byte TC_REFERENCE;
    final static byte TC_CLASSDESC;
    final static byte TC_OBJECT;
    final static byte TC_STRING;
    final static byte TC_ARRAY;
    final static byte TC_CLASS;
    final static byte TC_BLOCKDATA;
    final static byte TC_ENDBLOCKDATA;
    final static byte TC_RESET;
    final static byte TC_BLOCKDATALONG;
    final static byte TC_EXCEPTION;
    final static byte TC_MAX;
    final static int baseWireHandle;
    final static byte SC_WRRD_METHODS;
    final static byte SC_SERIALIZABLE;
    final static byte SC_EXTERNALIZABLE;
```

java.io.OutputStream

OutputStream is the top of the "output" classes. You can't create an instance of this class — someone else gives it to you. You can use it directly if you like, but most programmers use other classes, such as DataOutputStream or PrintStream.

```
public abstract class OutputStream
    public void close() throws IOException
    public void flush() throws IOException
    public abstract void write(int b) throws IOException;
    public void write(byte b[]) throws IOException
    public void write(byte b[], int off, int len) throws
      IOException
```

java.io.OutputStreamWriter

This class is the bridge between OutputStream and Writer. OutputStream is an arbitrary stream for writing, whereas Writer is a character-based stream.

```
public class OutputStreamWriter extends Writer
    public void close() throws IOException
    public void flush() throws IOException
    void flushBuffer() throws IOException
    public String getEncoding()
    public OutputStreamWriter(OutputStream out, String enc)
        throws UnsupportedEncodingException
    public OutputStreamWriter(OutputStream out)
    public void write(int c) throws IOException
    public void write(char cbuf[], int off, int len) throws
        IOException
    public void write(String str, int off, int len) throws
        IOException
```

java.io.PipedInputStream

PipedInputStream allows two threads to communicate via a stream. This class reads bytes from a PipedOutputStream.

```
public class PipedInputStream extends InputStream
    boolean closed;
    boolean closedByReader;
    boolean connected;
    Thread readSide;
    Thread writeSide;
    protected static final int PIPE_SIZE;
    protected byte buffer[];
    protected int in;
    protected int out;
    public synchronized int available() throws IOException
    public void close() throws IOException
    public void connect(PipedOutputStream src) throws
        IOException
    public PipedInputStream(PipedOutputStream src) throws
        IOException
    public PipedInputStream()
    public synchronized int read() throws IOException
    public synchronized int read(byte b[], int off, int len)
        throws IOException
    protected synchronized void receive(int b) throws
        IOException
    synchronized void receive(byte b[], int off, int len) throws
        IOException
    synchronized void receivedLast()
```

java.io.PipedOutputStream

PipedOutputStream allows two threads to communicate via a stream. This class writes bytes to a PipedInputStream.

```
public class PipedOutputStream extends OutputStream
    boolean connected;
```

```
public void close() throws IOException
public void connect(PipedInputStream snk) throws IOException
public synchronized void flush() throws IOException
public PipedOutputStream(PipedInputStream snk) throws
    IOException
public PipedOutputStream()
public void write(int b) throws IOException
public void write(byte b[], int off, int len) throws
    IOException
```

java.io.PipedReader

This class allows two threads to communicate via a character stream. `PipedReader` resembles `PipedInputStream`, except that it works with characters instead of bytes.

```
public class PipedReader extends Reader

    PipedInputStream byteSink;
    public void close() throws IOException
    public void connect(PipedWriter src) throws IOException
    public PipedReader()
    public PipedReader(PipedWriter src) throws IOException
    public int read(char cbuf[], int off, int len) throws
        IOException
```

java.io.PipedWriter

This class allows two threads to communicate via a character stream. `PipedWriter` differs from `PipedOutStream` in that it works on characters instead of bytes.

```
public class PipedWriter extends Writer

    PipedOutputStream byteSource;
    public void close() throws IOException
    public void connect(PipedReader sink) throws IOException
    public void flush() throws IOException
    public PipedWriter()
    public PipedWriter(PipedReader sink) throws IOException
    public void write(char cbuf[], int off, int len) throws
        IOException
```

java.io.PrintStream

You find the venerable `println()` method in `PrintStream`, a simple output stream with several "print" methods.

```
public class PrintStream extends FilterOutputStream

    public boolean checkError()
    public void close()
    public void flush()
    public void print(boolean b)
    public void print(char c)
    public void print(int i)
    public void print(long l)
    public void print(float f)
```

(continued)

(continued)

```
public void print(double d)
public void print(char s[])
public void print(String s)
public void print(Object obj)
public void println()
public void println(boolean x)
public void println(char x)
public void println(int x)
public void println(long x)
public void println(float x)
public void println(double x)
public void println(char x[])
public void println(String x)
public void println(Object x)
public PrintStream(OutputStream out)
public PrintStream(OutputStream out, boolean autoFlush)
protected void setError()
public void write(int b)
public void write(byte buf[], int off, int len)
```

java.io.PrintWriter

PrintWriter resembles PrintStream, but it works on character streams.

```
public class PrintWriter extends Writer
    public boolean checkError()
    public void close()
    public void flush()
    public void print(boolean b)
    public void print(char c)
    public void print(int i)
    public void print(long l)
    public void print(float f)
    public void print(double d)
    public void print(char s[])
    public void print(String s)
    public void print(Object obj)
    public void println()
    public void println(boolean x)
    public void println(char x)
    public void println(int x)
    public void println(long x)
    public void println(float x)
    public void println(double x)
    public void println(char x[])
    public void println(String x)
    public void println(Object x)
    public PrintWriter(Writer out)
    public PrintWriter(Writer out, boolean autoFlush)
    public PrintWriter(OutputStream out)
    public PrintWriter(OutputStream out, boolean autoFlush)
    protected void setError()
    public void write(int c)
    public void write(char buf[], int off, int len)
    public void write(char buf[])
    public void write(String s, int off, int len)
    public void write(String s)
```

java.io.PushbackInputStream

`PushbackInputStream` implements an input stream filter that lets you "push back" bytes that have previously been read. Basically, if you bite off more than you can chew, this class helps you put some back on the plate.

```
public class PushbackInputStream extends FilterInputStream
    protected byte[] buf;
    protected int pos;
    public int available() throws IOException
    public boolean markSupported()
    public PushbackInputStream(InputStream in, int size)
    public PushbackInputStream(InputStream in)
    public int read() throws IOException
    public int read(byte[] b, int off, int len) throws
        IOException
    public void unread(int b) throws IOException
    public void unread(byte[] b, int off, int len) throws
        IOException
    public void unread(byte[] b) throws IOException
```

java.io.PushbackReader

This class implements a `Reader` stream filter that lets you "push back" characters that have previously been read.

```
public class PushbackReader extends FilterReader
    public void close() throws IOException
    public boolean markSupported()
    public PushbackReader(Reader in, int size)
    public PushbackReader(Reader in)
    public int read() throws IOException
    public int read(char cbuf[], int off, int len) throws
        IOException
    public boolean ready() throws IOException
    public void unread(int c) throws IOException
    public void unread(char cbuf[], int off, int len) throws
        IOException
    public void unread(char cbuf[]) throws IOException
```

java.io.RandomAccessFile

The file stream `RandomAccessFile` allows reading, writing, and seeking.

```
public class RandomAccessFile implements DataOutput, DataInput
    public native void close() throws IOException;
    public final FileDescriptor getFD() throws IOException
    public native long getFilePointer() throws IOException;
    public native long length() throws IOException;
    public RandomAccessFile(String name, String mode) throws
        IOException
    public RandomAccessFile(File file, String mode) throws
        IOException
    public native int read() throws IOException;
```

(continued)

(continued)

```
public int read(byte b[], int off, int len) throws
    IOException
public int read(byte b[]) throws IOException
public final boolean readBoolean() throws IOException
public final byte readByte() throws IOException
public final char readChar() throws IOException
public final double readDouble() throws IOException
public final float readFloat() throws IOException
public final void readFully(byte b[]) throws IOException
public final void readFully(byte b[], int off, int len)
    throws IOException
public final int readInt() throws IOException
public final String readLine() throws IOException
public final long readLong() throws IOException
public final short readShort() throws IOException
public final int readUnsignedByte() throws IOException
public final int readUnsignedShort() throws IOException
public final String readUTF() throws IOException
public native void seek(long pos) throws IOException;
public int skipBytes(int n) throws IOException
public native void write(int b) throws IOException;
public void write(byte b[]) throws IOException
public void write(byte b[], int off, int len) throws
    IOException
public final void writeBoolean(boolean v) throws IOException
public final void writeByte(int v) throws IOException
public final void writeBytes(String s) throws IOException
public final void writeChar(int v) throws IOException
public final void writeChars(String s) throws IOException
public final void writeDouble(double v) throws IOException
public final void writeFloat(float v) throws IOException
public final void writeInt(int v) throws IOException
public final void writeLong(long v) throws IOException
public final void writeShort(int v) throws IOException
public final void writeUTF(String str) throws IOException
```

java.io.Reader

Reader is the top of the Reader classes. You can't create an instance of this class — someone else gives it to you. You can use it directly if you like, but it's more common to use other classes, such as DataReader.

```
public abstract class Reader
    protected Object lock;
    abstract public void close() throws IOException;
    public void mark(int readAheadLimit) throws IOException
    public boolean markSupported()
    public int read() throws IOException
    public int read(char cbuf[]) throws IOException
    abstract public int read(char cbuf[], int off, int len)
        throws IOException;
    protected Reader()
    protected Reader(Object lock)
    public boolean ready() throws IOException
    public void reset() throws IOException
    public long skip(long n) throws IOException
```

java.io.SequenceInputStream

SequenceInputStream lets you read from a sequence of streams. The class reads from the first stream until it encounters end-of-file, and then it closes the first stream and continues with the second.

```
public class SequenceInputStream extends InputStream

    Enumeration e;
    InputStream in;
    public int available() throws IOException
    public void close() throws IOException
    final void nextStream() throws IOException
    public int read() throws IOException
    public int read(byte buf[], int pos, int len) throws
        IOException
    public SequenceInputStream(Enumeration e)
    public SequenceInputStream(InputStream s1, InputStream s2)
```

java.io.Serializable

Classes that can be serialized use this interface.

```
public interface Serializable
```

java.io.StreamTokenizer

If you need your stream broken up into more readable pieces, then you can call on StreamTokenizer to parse your stream. StreamTokenizer functions much like StringTokenizer, but StreamTokenizer (obviously) works on streams.

```
public class StreamTokenizer

    public int ttype;
    public static final int TT_EOF;
    public static final int TT_EOL;
    public static final int TT_NUMBER;
    public static final int TT_WORD;
    public String sval;
    public double nval;
    public void commentChar(int ch)
    public void eolIsSignificant(boolean flag)
    public int lineno()
    public void lowerCaseMode(boolean fl)
    public int nextToken() throws IOException
    public void ordinaryChar(int ch)
    public void ordinaryChars(int low, int hi)
    public void parseNumbers()
    public void pushBack()
    public void quoteChar(int ch)
    public void resetSyntax()
    public void slashSlashComments(boolean flag)
    public void slashStarComments(boolean flag)
    public StreamTokenizer(InputStream I)
    public StreamTokenizer(Reader I)
    public String toString()
    public void whitespaceChars(int low, int hi)
    public void wordChars(int low, int hi)
```

java.io.StringBufferInputStream

The name of this simple class rivals some German words in length and complexity (although the German word for unemployment insurance, *Arbeitslosigkeitsversicherung*, may still have it beat by a hair). After you conquer how to say the class's name, you can use it to read bytes into a String object.

```
public class StringBufferInputStream extends InputStream
    protected String buffer;
    protected int pos;
    protected int count;
    public synchronized int available()
    public synchronized int read()
    public synchronized int read(byte b[], int off, int len)
    public synchronized void reset()
    public synchronized long skip(long n)
    public StringBufferInputStream(String s)
```

java.io.StringReader

StringReader reads characters into a String object.

```
public class StringReader extends Reader
    public void close()
    public void mark(int readAheadLimit) throws IOException
    public boolean markSupported()
    public int read() throws IOException
    public int read(char cbuf[], int off, int len) throws
        IOException
    public boolean ready()
    public void reset() throws IOException
    public long skip(long ns) throws IOException
    public StringReader(String s)
```

java.io.StringWriter

You may already be familiar with some string writers (Mozart, Stravinski, and Bach may come to mind). You may be a little less familiar with StringWriter, a graceful class that writes characters from a String object.

```
public class StringWriter extends Writer
    public void close()
    public void flush()
    public StringBuffer getBuffer()
    public StringWriter()
    protected StringWriter(int initialSize)
    public String toString()
    public void write(int c)
    public void write(char cbuf[], int off, int len)
    public void write(String str)
    public void write(String str, int off, int len)
```

java.io.Writer

You have reached the top of the "Writer" classes. Someone else gives you an instance of this class — you can't create it. You can use `Writer` directly if you like, but it's more common to use other classes, such as `DataWriter`.

```
public abstract class Writer

    protected Object lock;
    abstract public void close() throws IOException;
    abstract public void flush() throws IOException;
    public void write(int c) throws IOException
    public void write(char cbuf[]) throws IOException
    abstract public void write(char cbuf[], int off, int len)
        throws IOException;
    public void write(String str) throws IOException
    public void write(String str, int off, int len) throws
        IOException
    protected Writer()
    protected Writer(Object lock)
```

The java.lang Package

The `java.lang` package contains all the fundamental classes that make up the Java language. This package contains classes that every program, no matter how simple or complex, will have to use. In fact, the `java.lang` package is the only package that doesn't require an explicit import statement.

The `java.lang` package contains the all-important `Object` and `Class` classes. Every class in Java must extend another class. If you create a class and do not explicitly extend a class, your class extends `Object` by default. `Object` is therefore the superclass of every class in Java. When a class is used, a `Class` object must be created at run time. `Class` represents Java classes at run time.

Frequently, you need to represent a value of a primitive type as if it were an object or a reference type. The wrapper classes, including `Boolean`, `Byte`, `Character`, `Double`, `Float`, `Integer`, `Long`, and `Short`, allow a primitive data type to be stored and referenced as an object.

Remember: A primitive type is always passed to a method by copy, and an object is always passed by reference. The classes in this package are very helpful if you want to pass a primitive value to a method by reference.

TIP

Look in the wrapper classes for a number of methods to convert among the primitive types or from a `String`. For example, the `Integer` class contains a `parseInt()` method to convert a `String` to int.

The Math class provides commonly used mathematical functions, such as sine, cosine, and square root. The classes String and StringBuffer also provide commonly used operations on character strings.

The classes ClassLoader, Process, Runtime, SecurityManager, and System provide "system operations" that manage the dynamic loading of classes, creation of external processes, host environment inquiries (such as the time of day), and enforcing security policies.

The Throwableclass encompasses objects that may be thrown by the throw statement. Subclasses of Throwable represent errors and exceptions (see Part IV for more information on errors and exceptions).

The following figure shows you the hierarchy of classes defined in the java.lang package:

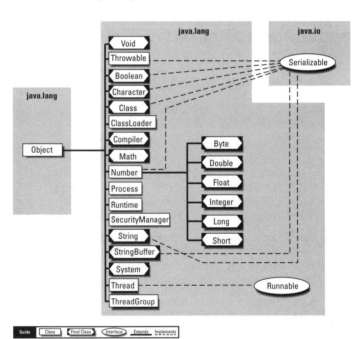

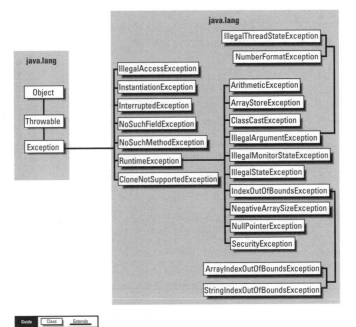

java.lang.Boolean

Boolean reigns as the king of "true" and "false." The Boolean class provides an object wrapper for boolean data values. You may find Boolean very handy because many of Java's utility classes require the use of objects. Because booleans are not objects in Java, they need to be "wrapped" in a Boolean instance.

```
public final class Boolean implements java.io.Serializable
    public static final Boolean TRUE;
    public static final Boolean FALSE;
    public static final Class TYPE;
    public Boolean(boolean value)
    public Boolean(String s)
    public boolean booleanValue()
    public boolean equals(Object obj)
    public static boolean getBoolean(String name)
    public int hashCode()
    public String toString()
    public static Boolean valueOf(String s)
```

java.lang.Byte

Use this standard wrapper for byte values when you need to pass a byte value by reference.

```
public final class Byte extends Number
    public static final byte MIN_VALUE;
    public static final byte MAX_VALUE;
    public static final Class TYPE;
    public Byte(byte value)
    public Byte(String s) throws NumberFormatException
    public byte byteValue()
    public static Byte decode(String nm) throws
        NumberFormatException
    public double doubleValue()
    public boolean equals(Object obj)
    public float floatValue()
    public int hashCode()
    public int intValue()
    public long longValue()
    public static byte parseByte(String s) throws
        NumberFormatException
    public static byte parseByte(String s, int radix) throws
        NumberFormatException
    public short shortValue()
    public static String toString(byte b)
    public String toString()
    public static Byte valueOf(String s, int radix) throws
        NumberFormatException
    public static Byte valueOf(String s) throws
        NumberFormatException
```

java.lang.Character

When you need to pass a char value by reference, the Character class provides an object wrapper for the primitive char data type.

```
public final class Character extends Object implements
java.io.Serializable
    public static final int MIN_RADIX;
    public static final int MAX_RADIX;
    public static final char MIN_VALUE;
    public static final char MAX_VALUE;
    public static final Class TYPE;
    public static final byte UNASSIGNED;
    public Character(char value)
    public char charValue()
    public static int digit(char ch, int radix)
    public boolean equals(Object obj)
    public static char forDigit(int digit, int radix)
    public static int getNumericValue(char ch)
    public static int getType(char ch)
    public int hashCode()
    public static boolean isDefined(char ch)
    public static boolean isDigit(char ch)
    public static boolean isIdentifierIgnorable(char ch)
    public static boolean isISOControl(char ch)
    public static boolean isJavaIdentifierPart(char ch)
    public static boolean isJavaIdentifierStart(char ch)
```

```
public static boolean isJavaLetter(char ch)
public static boolean isJavaLetterOrDigit(char ch)
public static boolean isLetter(char ch)
public static boolean isLetterOrDigit(char ch)
public static boolean isLowerCase(char ch)
public static boolean isSpace(char ch)
public static boolean isSpaceChar(char ch)
public static boolean isTitleCase(char ch)
public static boolean isUnicodeIdentifierPart(char ch)
public static boolean isUnicodeIdentifierStart(char ch)
public static boolean isUpperCase(char ch)
public static boolean isWhitespace(char ch)
public static char toLowerCase(char ch)
public String toString()
public static char toTitleCase(char ch)
public static char toUpperCase(char ch)
```

java.lang.Class

Instances of Class represent classes and interfaces so that they can be manipulated by a running Java program. Every array also belongs to a class represented by a Class object; all arrays with the same element type and number of dimensions share the Class object.

Class offers no public constructor, but the class method forName() returns a Class object. The Java virtual machine automatically constructs Class objects when classes are loaded; user programs can't create such objects.

```
public final class Class implements java.io.Serializable
    public static native Class forName(String className) throws
        ClassNotFoundException;
    public Class[] getClasses()
    public native ClassLoader getClassLoader();
    public native Class getComponentType();
    public Constructor getConstructor(Class[] parameterTypes)
        throws NoSuchMethodException, SecurityException
    public Constructor[] getConstructors() throws
        SecurityException
    public Class[] getDeclaredClasses() throws SecurityException
    public Constructor getDeclaredConstructor(Class[]
        parameterTypes) throws NoSuchMethodException,
        SecurityException
    public Constructor[] getDeclaredConstructors() throws
        SecurityException
    public Field getDeclaredField(String name) throws
        NoSuchFieldException, SecurityException
    public Field[] getDeclaredFields() throws SecurityException
    public Method getDeclaredMethod(String name, Class[]
        parameterTypes) throws NoSuchMethodException,
        SecurityException
    public Method[] getDeclaredMethods() throws
        SecurityException
    public Class getDeclaringClass()
    public Field getField(String name) throws
        NoSuchFieldException, SecurityException
    public Field[] getFields() throws SecurityException
```

(continued)

(continued)

```
public native Class[] getInterfaces();
public Method getMethod(String name, Class[] parameterTypes)
    throws NoSuchMethodException, SecurityException
public Method[] getMethods() throws SecurityException
public native int getModifiers();
public native String getName();
static native Class getPrimitiveClass(String name);
public java.net.URL getResource(String name)
public InputStream getResourceAsStream(String name)
public native Object[] getSigners();
public native Class getSuperclass();
public native boolean isArray();
public native boolean isAssignableFrom(Class cls);
public native boolean isInstance(Object obj);
public native boolean isInterface();
public native boolean isPrimitive();
public native Object newInstance() throws
    InstantiationException, IllegalAccessException;
native void setSigners(Object[] signers);
public String toString()
```

java.lang.ClassLoader

ClassLoader, an abstract class, defines a policy for loading Java classes into the run-time environment.

 For most applications, you won't need to define a policy for loading Java classes into the run-time environment. We usually let the Java run time handle that itself.

```
public abstract class ClassLoader

    protected ClassLoader()
    protected final Class defineClass(byte data[], int offset,
        int length)
    protected final Class defineClass(String name, byte data[],
        int offset, int length)
    final protected Class findLoadedClass(String name)
    protected final Class findSystemClass(String name) throws
        ClassNotFoundException
    public java.net.URL getResource(String name)
    public InputStream getResourceAsStream(String name)
    public static final java.net.URL getSystemResource(String
        name)
    public static final InputStream
        getSystemResourceAsStream(String name)
    public Class loadClass(String name) throws
        ClassNotFoundException
    protected abstract Class loadClass(String name, boolean
        resolve) throws ClassNotFoundException;
    final Class loadClassInternal(String name, boolean resolve)
        throws ClassNotFoundException
    protected final void resolveClass(Class c)
    protected final void setSigners(Class cl, Object[] signers)
```

java.lang.Cloneable

The Cloneable interface indicates that a class can be cloned (copied) by calling the Object method clone(). The interface contains no methods or variables. Because objects are always passed to methods by reference, the method can modify the original objects data. If you want the method to receive its own copy of the object, you would have to clone it first.

If `clone()` is called for an object that does not implement `Cloneable`, a `CloneNotSupportedException` will be thrown.

```
public interface Cloneable
```

java.lang.Compiler

The methods in this class provide access to the Java compiler. The `Compiler` class supports Java-to-native-code compilers and related services. By design, the `Compiler` class does nothing; it serves as a placeholder for a JIT (Just In Time) compiler implementation.

```
public final class Compiler
    public static native Object command(Object any);
    public static native boolean compileClass(Class clazz);
    public static native boolean compileClasses(String string);
    public static native void disable();
    public static native void enable();
```

java.lang.Double

The `Double` class provides an object wrapper for the primitive `double` type. Use this object wrapper when you need to pass a double value by reference.

This class provides many methods to return a `Double` value as one of many primitives or to convert a `String` to a double. The class also provides many useful static constants. Two very useful constants are `MAX_VALUE` and `MIN_VALUE`, which represent the maximum and minimum values of a double value.

```
public final class Double extends Number
    public static final double POSITIVE_INFINITY;
    public static final double NEGATIVE_INFINITY;
    public static final double NaN;
    public static final double MAX_VALUE;
    public static final double MIN_VALUE;
    public static final Class TYPE;
    public byte byteValue()
    public Double(double value)
    public Double(String s) throws NumberFormatException
    public static native long doubleToLongBits(double value);
    public double doubleValue()
    public boolean equals(Object obj)
    public float floatValue()
    public int hashCode()
    public int intValue()
    static public boolean isInfinite(double v)
```

(continued)

(continued)

```
public boolean isInfinite()
static public boolean isNaN(double v)
public boolean isNaN()
public static native double longBitsToDouble(long bits);
public long longValue()
public short shortValue()
public static String toString(double d)
public String toString()
public static Double valueOf(String s) throws
    NumberFormatException
static native double valueOf0(String s) throws
    NumberFormatException;
```

java.lang.Float

The Float class provides an object wrapper for the primitive float type. Use this wrapper when you need to pass a float value by reference.

This class provides many methods to return a float value as one of many primitives or to convert a String to a float. The class also provides many useful static constants. Two very useful constants are MAX_VALUE and MIN_VALUE, which represent the maximum and minimum values of a float value.

```
public final class Float extends Number
    public static final float POSITIVE_INFINITY;
    public static final float NEGATIVE_INFINITY;
    public static final float NaN;
    public static final float MAX_VALUE;
    public static final float MIN_VALUE;
    public static final Class TYPE;
    public byte byteValue()
    public double doubleValue()
    public boolean equals(Object obj)
    public Float(float value)
    public Float(double value)
    public Float(String s) throws NumberFormatException
    public static native int floatToIntBits(float value);
    public float floatValue()
    public int hashCode()
    public static native float intBitsToFloat(int bits);
    public int intValue()
    static public boolean isInfinite(float v)
    public boolean isInfinite()
    static public boolean isNaN(float v)
    public boolean isNaN()
    public long longValue()
    public short shortValue()
    public static String toString(float f)
    public String toString()
    public static Float valueOf(String s) throws
        NumberFormatException
```

java.lang.Integer

The Integer class provides an object wrapper for the primitive int type. Integer is useful when you need to pass an int value by reference. This class provides many methods to return an Integer value as one of many primitives. The class also provides many useful static constants. Two very useful constants are MAX_VALUE and MIN_VALUE, which represent the maximum and minimum values of an int value.

```
public final class Integer extends Number
    public static final int MIN_VALUE;
    public static final int MAX_VALUE;
    public static final Class TYPE;
    public byte byteValue()
    public static Integer decode(String nm) throws
        NumberFormatException
    public double doubleValue()
    public boolean equals(Object obj)
    public float floatValue()
    public static Integer getInteger(String nm)
    public static Integer getInteger(String nm, int val)
    public static Integer getInteger(String nm, Integer val)
    public int hashCode()
    public Integer(int value)
    public Integer(String s) throws NumberFormatException
    public int intValue()
    public long longValue()
    public static int parseInt(String s, int radix) throws
        NumberFormatException
    public static int parseInt(String s) throws
        NumberFormatException
    public short shortValue()
    public static String toBinaryString(int i)
    public static String toHexString(int i)
    public static String toOctalString(int i)
    public static String toString(int i, int radix)
    public static String toString(int i)
    public String toString()
    public static Integer valueOf(String s, int radix) throws
        NumberFormatException
    public static Integer valueOf(String s) throws
        NumberFormatException
```

java.lang.Long

The Long class provides an object wrapper for the primitive long type; yes, we know how exciting that can be. All kidding aside, we promise that you will thank the Java powers-that-be for this class when you need to pass a long value by reference. This class provides many methods to return a long value as one of many primitives. The class also provides many useful static constants, such as MAX_VALUE and MIN_VALUE, which represent the maximum and minimum values of a long value.

```
public final class Long extends Number
    public static final long MIN_VALUE;
    public static final long MAX_VALUE;
    public static final Class TYPE;
    public byte byteValue()
    public double doubleValue()
    public boolean equals(Object obj)
    public float floatValue()
    public static Long getLong(String nm)
    public static Long getLong(String nm, long val)
    public static Long getLong(String nm, Long val)
    public int hashCode()
    public int intValue()
    public Long(long value)
    public Long(String s) throws NumberFormatException
    public long longValue()
    public static long parseLong(String s, int radix) throws
        NumberFormatException
    public static long parseLong(String s) throws
        NumberFormatException
    public short shortValue()
    public static String toBinaryString(long i)
    public static String toHexString(long i)
    public static String toOctalString(long i)
    public static String toString(long i, int radix)
    public static String toString(long i)
    public String toString()
    public static Long valueOf(String s, int radix) throws
        NumberFormatException
    public static Long valueOf(String s) throws
        NumberFormatException
```

java.lang.Math

The Math class provides a standard Math library. Math defines constants for values e and pi and various methods for evaluating mathematical functions.

All the methods and variables in Math are static and are called or referenced by the class name (Math). Math can't be subclassed or instantiated because all methods and variables are static.

TIP

The Java language doesn't offer a built-in exponentiation operator; however, you can still exponentiate by using the pow() method in the Math class. For example, Math.pow(a,b) returns a raised to the power of b.

```
public final class Math
    public static final double E;
    public static final double PI;
    public static int abs(int a)
    public static long abs(long a)
    public static float abs(float a)
    public static double abs(double a)
    public static native double acos(double a);
    public static native double asin(double a);
    public static native double atan(double a);
    public static native double atan2(double a, double b);
    public static native double ceil(double a);
    public static native double cos(double a);
```

```
public static native double exp(double a);
public static native double floor(double a);
public static native double IEEEremainder(double f1, double
    f2);
public static native double log(double a);
public static int max(int a, int b)
public static long max(long a, long b)
public static float max(float a, float b)
public static double max(double a, double b)
public static int min(int a, int b)
public static long min(long a, long b)
public static float min(float a, float b)
public static double min(double a, double b)
public static native double pow(double a, double b);
public static synchronized double random()
public static native double rint(double a);
public static int round(float a)
public static long round(double a)
public static native double sin(double a);
public static native double sqrt(double a);
public static native double tan(double a);
```

java.lang.Number

Number, an abstract class, represents the superclass for the numeric scalar types Byte, Integer, Long, Float Double, and Short. Number defines conversion methods that all those types must implement.

```
public abstract class Number implements java.io.Serializable
    public byte byteValue()
    public abstract double doubleValue();
    public abstract float floatValue();
    public abstract int intValue();
    public abstract long longValue();
    public short shortValue()
```

java.lang.Object

Object is the single root of the class hierarchy. All objects, including arrays, implement the methods of this class.

You should override many of the Object methods by all sub-classes. Yes, that means every class you make — yes, you. All classes should provide a toString() method to ensure proper operation of the string concatenation, making your class more useful and easier to debug at 3:00 a.m.

```
public class Object
    protected native Object clone() throws
        CloneNotSupportedException;
    public boolean equals(Object obj)
    protected void finalize() throws Throwable
    public final native Class getClass();
    public native int hashCode();
    public final native void notify();
    public final native void notifyAll();
```

(continued)

(continued)

```
public String toString()
public final native void wait(long timeout) throws
  InterruptedException;
public final void wait(long timeout, int nanos) throws
  InterruptedException
public final void wait() throws InterruptedException
```

java.lang.Process

This abstract class describes a process returned by variants of the exec() method in System — Runtime.exec(), for example. The Process instance allows you access to the standard in and/or standard out of the subprocess, to kill the subprocess, to wait for the subprocess to terminate, and to retrieve the final exit value of the process.

TIP

Dropping the last reference to a Process instance does not kill the subprocess. The subprocess doesn't have to execute asynchronously with the existing Java process.

```
public abstract class Process
    abstract public void destroy();
    abstract public int exitValue();
    abstract public InputStream getErrorStream();
    abstract public InputStream getInputStream();
    abstract public OutputStream getOutputStream();
    abstract public int waitFor() throws InterruptedException;
```

java.lang.Runnable

This interface specifies the run() method required for a thread. A class can be created as a thread by either extending the Thread class or implementing Runnable.

```
public interface Runnable
    public abstract void run();
```

java.lang.Runtime

Runtime executes other, possibly non-Java, programs. Runtime launches native applications from your Java program. To run a native application, first you must obtain a Runtime object; the static method getRuntime() returns one. With that object, you can then use the exec() method and pass it the path and name of the application you would like to start.

```
public class Runtime
    public Process exec(String command) throws IOException
    public Process exec(String command, String envp[]) throws
      IOException
    public Process exec(String cmdarray[]) throws IOException
    public Process exec(String cmdarray[], String envp[]) throws
      IOException
```

```
public void exit(int status)
public native long freeMemory();
public native void gc();
public InputStream getLocalizedInputStream(InputStream in)
public OutputStream getLocalizedOutputStream(OutputStream
    out)
public static Runtime getRuntime()
public synchronized void load(String filename)
public synchronized void loadLibrary(String libname)
public native void runFinalization();
public static void runFinalizersOnExit(boolean value)
public native long totalMemory();
public native void traceInstructions(boolean on);
public native void traceMethodCalls(boolean on);
```

java.lang.SecurityManager

SecurityManager, an abstract class, can be subclassed to create
a security policy for the execution of untrusted code.
SecurityManager allows the inspection of the classloaders on
the execution stack.

```
public abstract class SecurityManager

    protected boolean inCheck;
    public void checkAccept(String host, int port)
    public void checkAccess(Thread g)
    public void checkAccess(ThreadGroup g)
    public void checkAwtEventQueueAccess()
    public void checkConnect(String host, int port)
    public void checkConnect(String host, int port, Object
        context)
    public void checkCreateClassLoader()
    public void checkDelete(String file)
    public void checkExec(String cmd)
    public void checkExit(int status)
    public void checkLink(String lib)
    public void checkListen(int port)
    public void checkMemberAccess(Class clazz, int which)
    public void checkMulticast(InetAddress maddr)
    public void checkMulticast(InetAddress maddr, byte ttl)
    public void checkPackageAccess(String pkg)
    public void checkPackageDefinition(String pkg)
    public void checkPrintJobAccess()
    public void checkPropertiesAccess()
    public void checkPropertyAccess(String key)
    public void checkRead(FileDescriptor fd)
    public void checkRead(String file)
    public void checkRead(String file, Object context)
    public void checkSecurityAccess(String provider)
    public void checkSetFactory()
    public void checkSystemClipboardAccess()
    public boolean checkTopLevelWindow(Object window)
    public void checkWrite(FileDescriptor fd)
    public void checkWrite(String file)
    protected native int classDepth(String name);
    protected native int classLoaderDepth();
    protected native ClassLoader currentClassLoader();
    protected Class currentLoadedClass()
    protected native Class[] getClassContext();
    public boolean getInCheck()
```

(continued)

(continued)

```
public Object getSecurityContext()
public ThreadGroup getThreadGroup()
protected boolean inClass(String name)
protected boolean inClassLoader()
protected SecurityManager()
```

java.lang.Short

The Short class provides an object wrapper for the primitive short type. When you need to pass a short value by reference, the Short class steps in to do the job. This class provides many methods to return a short value as one of many primitives. The class also provides many useful static constants, including MAX_VALUE and MIN_VALUE, which represent the maximum and minimum values of a short value.

```
public final class Short extends Number
    public static final short MIN_VALUE;
    public static final short MAX_VALUE;
    public static final Class TYPE;
    public byte byteValue()
    public static Short decode(String nm) throws
        NumberFormatException
    public double doubleValue()
    public boolean equals(Object obj)
    public float floatValue()
    public int hashCode()
    public int intValue()
    public long longValue()
    public static short parseShort(String s) throws
        NumberFormatException
    public static short parseShort(String s, int radix) throws
        NumberFormatException
    public Short(short value)
    public Short(String s) throws NumberFormatException
    public short shortValue()
    public static String toString(short s)
    public String toString()
    public static Short valueOf(String s, int radix) throws
        NumberFormatException
    public static Short valueOf(String s) throws
        NumberFormatException
```

java.lang.String

The String class represents a character string. A String object is created whenever an applet encounters a string in double quotes.

When using String, you don't need a constructor and the new keyword. String objects are *immutable* (constant) and can't be changed after creation. If you want to manipulate the contents of a String, use StringBuffer.

TIP

You can concatenate `String` objects using the + operator, which automatically calls the object's `toString()` method. Use this clever shortcut to convert anything to a `String`:

```
String myString = "" + object;
```

```java
public final class String implements java.io.Serializable
    public char charAt(int index)
    public int compareTo(String anotherString)
    public String concat(String str)
    public static String copyValueOf(char data[], int offset,
        int count)
    public static String copyValueOf(char data[])
    public boolean endsWith(String suffix)
    public boolean equals(Object anObject)
    public boolean equalsIgnoreCase(String anotherString)
    public void getBytes(int srcBegin, int srcEnd, byte dst[],
        int dstBegin)
    public byte[] getBytes(String enc) throws
        UnsupportedEncodingException
    public byte[] getBytes()
    public void getChars(int srcBegin, int srcEnd, char dst[],
        int dstBegin)
    public int hashCode()
    public int indexOf(int ch)
    public int indexOf(int ch, int fromIndex)
    public int indexOf(String str)
    public int indexOf(String str, int fromIndex)
    public native String intern();
    public int lastIndexOf(int ch)
    public int lastIndexOf(int ch, int fromIndex)
    public int lastIndexOf(String str)
    public int lastIndexOf(String str, int fromIndex)
    public int length()
    public boolean regionMatches(int toffset, String other, int
        offset, int len)
    public boolean regionMatches(boolean ignoreCase, int
        offset, String other, int ooffset, int len)
    public String replace(char oldChar, char newChar)
    public boolean startsWith(String prefix, int toffset)
    public boolean startsWith(String prefix)
    public String()
    public String(String value)
    public String(char value[])
    public String(char value[], int offset, int count)
    public String(byte ascii[], int hibyte, int offset, int
        count)
    public String(byte ascii[], int hibyte)
    public String(byte bytes[], int offset, int length, String
        enc) throws UnsupportedEncodingException
    public String(byte bytes[], String enc) throws
        UnsupportedEncodingException
    public String(byte bytes[], int offset, int length)
    public String(byte bytes[])
    public String(StringBuffer buffer)
    public String substring(int beginIndex)
    public String substring(int beginIndex, int endIndex)
    public char[] toCharArray()
    public String toLowerCase( Locale locale )
```

(continued)

(continued)

```
public String toLowerCase()
public String toString()
public String toUpperCase( Locale locale )
public String toUpperCase()
public String trim()
int utfLength()
public static String valueOf(Object obj)
public static String valueOf(char data[])
public static String valueOf(char data[], int offset, int
    count)
public static String valueOf(boolean b)
public static String valueOf(char c)
public static String valueOf(int i)
public static String valueOf(long l)
public static String valueOf(float f)
public static String valueOf(double d)
```

java.lang.StringBuffer

The `StringBuffer` class represents a character string. Unlike the `String` class, you can modify the contents of `StringBuffer`. For example, you can modify the stored value with the `setCharAt()`, `append()`, and `insert()` methods.

If you need a `String` object that can change, use `StringBuffer` instead of `String`.

```
public final class StringBuffer implements java.io.Serializable
    static final long serialVersionUID;
    public synchronized StringBuffer append(Object obj)
    public synchronized StringBuffer append(String str)
    public synchronized StringBuffer append(char str[])
    public synchronized StringBuffer append(char str[], int
        offset, int len)
    public StringBuffer append(boolean b)
    public synchronized StringBuffer append(char c)
    public StringBuffer append(int i)
    public StringBuffer append(long l)
    public StringBuffer append(float f)
    public StringBuffer append(double d)
    public int capacity()
    public synchronized char charAt(int index)
    public synchronized void ensureCapacity(int minimumCapacity)
    public synchronized void getChars(int srcBegin, int srcEnd,
        char dst[], int dstBegin)
    final char[] getValue()
    public synchronized StringBuffer insert(int offset, Object
        obj)
    public synchronized StringBuffer insert(int offset, String
        str)
    public synchronized StringBuffer insert(int offset, char
        str[])
    public StringBuffer insert(int offset, boolean b)
    public synchronized StringBuffer insert(int offset, char c)
    public StringBuffer insert(int offset, int i)
    public StringBuffer insert(int offset, long l)
    public StringBuffer insert(int offset, float f)
    public StringBuffer insert(int offset, double d)
    public int length()
```

```
public synchronized StringBuffer reverse()
public synchronized void setCharAt(int index, char ch)
public synchronized void setLength(int newLength)
final void setShared()
public StringBuffer()
public StringBuffer(int length)
public StringBuffer(String str)
public String toString()
```

java.lang.System

The System class provides access to the venerable println() method, along with streams to stderr and stdin. System also offers methods to load shared objects to access native methods.

```
public final class System
    public final static InputStream in;
    public final static PrintStream out;
    public final static PrintStream err;
    public static native void arraycopy(Object src, int
        src_position, Object dst, int dst_position, int length);
    public static native long currentTimeMillis();
    public static void exit(int status)
    public static void gc()
    public static String getenv(String name)
    public static Properties getProperties()
    public static String getProperty(String key)
    public static String getProperty(String key, String def)
    public static SecurityManager getSecurityManager()
    public static native int identityHashCode(Object x);
    public static void load(String filename)
    public static void loadLibrary(String libname)
    public static void runFinalization()
    public static void runFinalizersOnExit(boolean value)
    public static void setErr(PrintStream err)
    public static void setIn(InputStream in)
    public static void setOut(PrintStream out)
    public static void setProperties(Properties props)
    public static void setSecurityManager(SecurityManager s)
```

java.lang.Thread

The Thread class creates separate threads. You can either extend this class or implement the Runnable interface to create a thread. In either case, you must define a run() method that can execute as a separate thread. Thread offers methods to modify and obtain a thread's priority and suspend execution.

```
public class Thread implements Runnable
    public final static int MIN_PRIORITY;
    public final static int NORM_PRIORITY;
    public final static int MAX_PRIORITY;
    public static int activeCount()
    public void checkAccess()
    public native int countStackFrames();
    public static native Thread currentThread();
```

(continued)

(continued)

```
public void destroy()
public static void dumpStack()
public static int enumerate(Thread tarray[])
public final String getName()
public final int getPriority()
public final ThreadGroup getThreadGroup()
public void interrupt()
public static boolean interrupted()
public final native boolean isAlive();
public final boolean isDaemon()
public boolean isInterrupted()
public final synchronized void join(long millis) throws
    InterruptedException
public final synchronized void join(long millis, int nanos)
    throws InterruptedException
public final void join() throws InterruptedException
public final void resume()
public void run()
public final void setDaemon(boolean on)
public final void setName(String name)
public final void setPriority(int newPriority)
public static native void sleep(long millis) throws
    InterruptedException;
public static void sleep(long millis, int nanos) throws
    InterruptedException
public synchronized native void start();
public final void stop()
public final synchronized void stop(Throwable o)
public final void suspend()
public Thread()
public Thread(Runnable target)
public Thread(ThreadGroup group, Runnable target)
public Thread(String name)
public Thread(ThreadGroup group, String name)
public Thread(Runnable target, String name)
public Thread(ThreadGroup group, Runnable target, String
    name)
public String toString()
public static native void yield();
```

java.lang.ThreadGroup

`ThreadGroup` helps you control several threads simultaneously — for example, the case of a Web server with multiple threads. `ThreadGroups` can contain `ThreadGroups` leading to a hierarchy of `Threads`.

```
public class ThreadGroup
    ThreadGroup parent;
    String name;
    int maxPriority;
    boolean destroyed;
    boolean daemon;
    boolean vmAllowSuspension;
    int nthreads;
    Thread threads[];
    int ngroups;
    ThreadGroup groups[];
    public int activeCount()
    public int activeGroupCount()
```

```
void add(Thread t)
public boolean allowThreadSuspension(boolean b)
public final void checkAccess()
public final void destroy()
public int enumerate(Thread list[])
public int enumerate(Thread list[], boolean recurse)
public int enumerate(ThreadGroup list[])
public int enumerate(ThreadGroup list[], boolean recurse)
public final int getMaxPriority()
public final String getName()
public final ThreadGroup getParent()
public final boolean isDaemon()
public synchronized boolean isDestroyed()
public void list()
void list(PrintStream out, int indent)
public final boolean parentOf(ThreadGroup g)
void remove(Thread t)
public final void resume()
public final void setDaemon(boolean daemon)
public final void setMaxPriority(int pri)
public final void stop()
public final void suspend()
public ThreadGroup(String name)
public ThreadGroup(ThreadGroup parent, String name)
public String toString()
public void uncaughtException(Thread t, Throwable e)
```

java.lang.Throwable

Throwable is no regular class. It's the superclass of all errors and exceptions. In order to create a class that can be thrown using the throw keyword, you must extend Throwable. (Take a look at Part IV for a discussion and hierarchy diagram of exceptions and errors subclassed from Throwable.)

```
public class Throwable implements java.io.Serializable
    public native Throwable fillInStackTrace();
    public String getLocalizedMessage()
    public String getMessage()
    public void printStackTrace()
    public void printStackTrace(java.io.PrintStream s)
    public void printStackTrace(java.io.PrintWriter s)
    public Throwable()
    public Throwable(String message)
    public String toString()
```

java.lang.Void

The Void class is anything but empty. Void, an uninstantiable placeholder class, holds a reference to the object representing the primitive Java type void. You can't instantiate this class because the constructor is marked private.

```
public final class Void
    public static final Class TYPE;
```

The java.net Package

The java.net package contains classes that build a strong base for networking. The java.net package supports Transmission Control Protocol (TCP) and User Datagram Protocol (UDP) sockets that you can use to create any type of client/server you desire. In addition, java.net provides specific classes for URL connections and HTTP URL connections, which can take you to locations on the World Wide Web.

Check out the amazing class hierarchy of this package in the following figure:

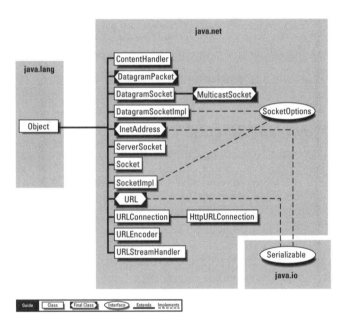

java.net.ContentHandler

ContentHandler, an abstract class, describes a URL content handler.

```
abstract public class ContentHandler
    abstract public Object getContent(URLConnection urlc) throws
        IOException;
```

java.net.ContentHandlerFactory

This abstract class describes an object that can create a URL content handler.

```
public interface ContentHandlerFactory
    ContentHandler createContentHandler(String mimetype);
```

java.net.DatagramPacket

Use this class to create a "packet" of data that can be sent or received through a `DatagramSocket`. This class has two constructors: The first creates a `DatagramPacket` with a byte array into which data can be received. The `receive()` method in the `DatagramSocket` class waits for and stores the data in this packet. The second constructor specifies a byte array and a destination address and port. Use the `send()` method in the `DatagramSocket` class to send this packet.

```
public final class DatagramPacket
    byte[] buf;
    int length;
    InetAddress address;
    int port;
    public DatagramPacket(byte ibuf[], int ilength)
    public DatagramPacket(byte ibuf[], int ilength, InetAddress
        iaddr, int iport)
    public InetAddress getAddress()
    public byte[] getData()
    public int getLength()
    public int getPort()
```

java.net.DatagramSocket

This class creates an unreliable datagram socket using the user datagram protocol (UDP). The `send()` and `receive()` methods send and receive `DatagramPacket`s (see "java.net.DatagramPacket" in this part for more information).

```
public class DatagramSocket
    DatagramSocketImpl impl;
    static Class implClass;
    public void close()
    public DatagramSocket() throws SocketException
    public DatagramSocket(int port) throws SocketException
    public DatagramSocket(int port, InetAddress laddr) throws
        SocketException
    public InetAddress getLocalAddress()
    public int getLocalPort()
    public synchronized int getSoTimeout() throws
        SocketException
    public synchronized void receive(DatagramPacket p) throws
        IOException
    public void send(DatagramPacket p) throws IOException
    public synchronized void setSoTimeout(int timeout) throws
        SocketException
    static
```

java.net.DatagramSocketImpl

DatagramSocketImpl, an abstract class, is a datagram and multicast socket implementation base class.

Remember: Abstract classes can't be instantiated directly; they must be subclassed.

```
public abstract class DatagramSocketImpl implements SocketOptions
    protected int localPort;
    protected FileDescriptor fd;
    protected abstract void bind(int lport, InetAddress laddr)
        throws SocketException;
    protected abstract void close();
    protected abstract void create() throws SocketException;
    protected FileDescriptor getFileDescriptor()
    protected int getLocalPort()
    protected abstract byte getTTL() throws IOException;
    protected abstract void join(InetAddress inetaddr) throws
        IOException;
    protected abstract void leave(InetAddress inetaddr) throws
        IOException;
    protected abstract int peek(InetAddress i) throws
        IOException;
    protected abstract void receive(DatagramPacket p) throws
        IOException;
    protected abstract void send(DatagramPacket p) throws
        IOException;
    protected abstract void setTTL(byte ttl) throws IOException;
```

java.net.FileNameMap

A simple interface that provides a mechanism to map between a file name and a MIME type string.

```
public interface FileNameMap
    public String getContentTypeFor(String fileName);
```

java.net.HttpURLConnection

HttpURLConnection extends URLConnection and adds HTTP specific features, such as SetRequestMethod(), which sets the HTTP request method to use. HttpURLConnection also defines numerous constants representing various HTTP status codes that can be transmitted or received.

HttpURLConnection extends URLConnection — look in that class for other functionalities.

```
abstract public class HttpURLConnection extends URLConnection
    protected String method;
    protected int responseCode;
    protected String responseMessage;
    public static final int HTTP_OK;
    public static final int HTTP_CREATED;
    public static final int HTTP_ACCEPTED;
    public static final int HTTP_NOT_AUTHORITATIVE;
```

```
public static final int HTTP_NO_CONTENT;
public static final int HTTP_RESET;
public static final int HTTP_PARTIAL;
public static final int HTTP_MULT_CHOICE;
public static final int HTTP_MOVED_PERM;
public static final int HTTP_MOVED_TEMP;
public static final int HTTP_SEE_OTHER;
public static final int HTTP_NOT_MODIFIED;
public static final int HTTP_USE_PROXY;
public static final int HTTP_BAD_REQUEST;
public static final int HTTP_UNAUTHORIZED;
public static final int HTTP_PAYMENT_REQUIRED;
public static final int HTTP_FORBIDDEN;
public static final int HTTP_NOT_FOUND;
public static final int HTTP_BAD_METHOD;
public static final int HTTP_NOT_ACCEPTABLE;
public static final int HTTP_PROXY_AUTH;
public static final int HTTP_CLIENT_TIMEOUT;
public static final int HTTP_CONFLICT;
public static final int HTTP_GONE;
public static final int HTTP_LENGTH_REQUIRED;
public static final int HTTP_PRECON_FAILED;
public static final int HTTP_ENTITY_TOO_LARGE;
public static final int HTTP_REQ_TOO_LONG;
public static final int HTTP_UNSUPPORTED_TYPE;
public static final int HTTP_SERVER_ERROR;
public static final int HTTP_INTERNAL_ERROR;
public static final int HTTP_BAD_GATEWAY;
public static final int HTTP_UNAVAILABLE;
public static final int HTTP_GATEWAY_TIMEOUT;
public static final int HTTP_VERSION;
public abstract void disconnect();
public static boolean getFollowRedirects()
public String getRequestMethod()
public int getResponseCode() throws IOException
public String getResponseMessage() throws IOException
protected HttpURLConnection(URL u)
public static void setFollowRedirects(boolean set)
public void setRequestMethod(String method) throws
    ProtocolException
public abstract boolean usingProxy();
```

java.net.InetAddress

InetAddress **represents an Internet address.**

```
public final class InetAddress implements java.io.Serializable
    String hostName;
    int address;
    int family;
    static Hashtable addressCache;
    static InetAddress unknownAddress;
    static InetAddress anyLocalAddress;
    static InetAddress localHost;
    static InetAddress[] unknown_array;
    static InetAddressImpl impl;
    public boolean equals(Object obj)
    public byte[] getAddress()
    public static InetAddress getAllByName(String host)[] throws
        UnknownHostException
```

(continued)

(continued)

```
public static InetAddress getByName(String host) throws
   UnknownHostException
public String getHostAddress()
public String getHostName()
public static InetAddress getLocalHost() throws
   UnknownHostException
public int hashCode()
InetAddress()
InetAddress(String hostName, byte addr[])
public boolean isMulticastAddress()
static
static
public String toString()
```

java.net.MulticastSocket

This class creates a multicast datagram socket for sending and receiving IP multicast packets. MulticastSocket extends (UDP) DatagramSocket, with additional capabilities for joining "groups" of other multicast hosts on the Internet.

You join a multicast group by first creating a MulticastSocket with the desired port and then invoking the joinGroup() method. When a socket subscribes to a multicast group/port, the socket receives datagrams sent by other hosts to the group/port, as do all other members of the group and port. When you send a message to a multicast group, all subscribing recipients to that host and port receive the message. A socket relinquishes membership in a group by the leaveGroup() method.

Currently, applets can't use multicast sockets; only applications have the privilege of enjoying a fine multicast socket.

```
public final class MulticastSocket extends DatagramSocket
   public InetAddress getInterface() throws SocketException
   public byte getTTL() throws IOException
   public void joinGroup(InetAddress mcastaddr) throws
      IOException
   public void leaveGroup(InetAddress mcastaddr) throws
      IOException
   public MulticastSocket() throws IOException
   public MulticastSocket(int port) throws IOException
   public synchronized void send(DatagramPacket p, byte ttl)
      throws IOException
   public void setInterface(InetAddress inf) throws
      SocketException
   public void setTTL(byte ttl) throws IOException
```

java.net.PlainDatagramSocketImpl

This class allows you to set socket options, such as time to live.

```
class PlainDatagramSocketImpl extends DatagramSocketImpl
   protected synchronized native void bind(int lport,
      InetAddress laddr) throws SocketException;
   protected void close()
```

```
protected synchronized void create() throws SocketException
protected synchronized void finalize()
public Object getOption(int optID) throws SocketException
protected native byte getTTL() throws IOException;
protected native void join(InetAddress inetaddr) throws
    IOException;
protected native void leave(InetAddress inetaddr) throws
    IOException;
protected synchronized native int peek(InetAddress i) throws
    IOException;
protected synchronized native void receive(DatagramPacket p)
    throws IOException;
protected synchronized native void send(DatagramPacket p)
    throws IOException;
public void setOption(int optID, Object o) throws
    SocketException
protected native void setTTL(byte ttl) throws IOException;
```

java.net.PlainSocketImpl

This class allows you to set socket options.

```
class PlainSocketImpl extends SocketImpl
    int timeout;
    public static final String socksServerProp;
    public static final String socksPortProp;
    public static final String socksDefaultPortStr;
    protected synchronized void accept(SocketImpl s) throws
        IOException
    protected synchronized int available() throws IOException
    protected synchronized void bind(InetAddress address, int
        lport) throws IOException
    protected void close() throws IOException
    protected void connect(String host, int port) throws
        UnknownHostException, IOException
    protected void connect(InetAddress address, int port) throws
        IOException
    protected synchronized void create(boolean stream) throws
        IOException
    protected void finalize() throws IOException
    protected synchronized InputStream getInputStream() throws
        IOException
    public Object getOption(int opt) throws SocketException
    protected synchronized OutputStream getOutputStream() throws
        IOException
    protected synchronized void listen(int count) throws
        IOException
    public void setOption(int opt, Object val) throws
        SocketException
```

java.net.ServerSocket

Use ServerSocket to create a server TCP socket. The most commonly used constructor accepts a port number, which creates a server socket that listens to the specified port number. The accept() method, a blocking method, listens and then waits for a client to connect.

ServerSocket uses a SocketImpl to implement the actual
socket operations so that you can change socket implementations
depending on the kind of firewall you use. You can change socket
implementations by setting the SocketImplFactory.

```
public class ServerSocket
    public Socket accept() throws IOException
    public void close() throws IOException
    public InetAddress getInetAddress()
    public int getLocalPort()
    public synchronized int getSoTimeout() throws IOException
    protected final void implAccept(Socket s) throws IOException
    public ServerSocket(int port) throws IOException
    public ServerSocket(int port, int backlog) throws
        IOException
    public ServerSocket(int port, int backlog, InetAddress
        bindAddr) throws IOException
    public static synchronized void
        setSocketFactory(SocketImplFactory fac) throws IOException
    public synchronized void setSoTimeout(int timeout) throws
        SocketException
    public String toString()
```

java.net.Socket

Socket creates a client TCP socket. The most commonly used
constructor accepts a host machine and port number, which
creates a socket connection to the specified machine at the
specified port number. The Socket class contains
getInputStream() and getOutputStream() methods that
return an InputStream and OutputStream, respectively. Data
can then be read using the InputStream and OutputStream
classes in the java.io package (see "The java.io Package" in this
part for more information).

Socket uses a SocketImpl to implement the actual socket
operations so that you can change socket implementations
depending on the kind of firewall you use. You can change socket
implementations by setting the SocketImplFactory.

```
public class Socket
    SocketImpl impl;
    private static SocketImplFactory factory;
    public InetAddress getInetAddress()
    public InputStream getInputStream() throws IOException
    public InetAddress getLocalAddress()
    public int getLocalPort()
    public OutputStream getOutputStream() throws IOException
    public int getPort()
    public int getSoLinger() throws SocketException
    public synchronized int getSoTimeout() throws
        SocketException
    public boolean getTcpNoDelay() throws SocketException
    public static synchronized void
```

```
setSocketImplFactory(SocketImplFactory fac) throws
  IOException
public void setSoLinger(boolean on, int val) throws
  SocketException
public synchronized void setSoTimeout(int timeout) throws
  SocketException
public void setTcpNoDelay(boolean on) throws SocketException
protected Socket()
protected Socket(SocketImpl impl) throws SocketException
public Socket(String host, int port) throws
  UnknownHostException, IOException
public Socket(InetAddress address, int port) throws
  IOException
public Socket(String host, int port, InetAddress localAddr,
  int localPort) throws IOException
public Socket(InetAddress address, int port, InetAddress
  localAddr, int localPort) throws IOException
public Socket(String host, int port, boolean stream) throws
  IOException
public Socket(InetAddress host, int port, boolean stream)
  throws IOException
public String toString()
```

java.net.SocketImpl

SocketImpl is the Socket implementation class. You need to subclass this abstract class to provide actual implementation to the socket. We know — it sounds painful, but it's not that bad. Trust us.

```
public abstract class SocketImpl implements SocketOptions
    protected FileDescriptor fd;
    protected InetAddress address;
    protected int port;
    protected int localport;
    protected abstract void accept(SocketImpl s) throws
      IOException;
    protected abstract int available() throws IOException;
    protected abstract void bind(InetAddress host, int port)
      throws IOException;
    protected abstract void close() throws IOException;
    protected abstract void connect(String host, int port)
      throws IOException;
    protected abstract void connect(InetAddress address, int
      port) throws IOException;
    protected abstract void create(boolean stream) throws
      IOException;
    protected FileDescriptor getFileDescriptor()
    protected InetAddress getInetAddress()
    protected abstract InputStream getInputStream() throws
      IOException;
    protected int getLocalPort()
    protected abstract OutputStream getOutputStream() throws
      IOException;
    protected int getPort()
    protected abstract void listen(int backlog) throws
      IOException;
    public String toString()
```

java.net.SocketImplFactory

This interface defines a factory for `SocketImpl` instances. The socket class uses `SocketImplFactory` to create socket implementations that implement various policies.

```
public interface SocketImplFactory
    SocketImpl createSocketImpl();
```

java.net.SocketOptions

This interface describes methods for setting BSD-style socket options.

```
interface SocketOptions
    public final static int TCP_NODELAY;
    public final static int SO_BINDADDR;
    public final static int SO_REUSEADDR;
    public final static int IP_MULTICAST_IF;
    public final static int SO_LINGER;
    public final static int SO_TIMEOUT;
    public Object getOption(int optID) throws SocketException;
    public void setOption(int optID, Object value) throws
        SocketException;
```

java.net.URL

Use this class to create a URL object that represents a *Uniform Resource Locator,* a resource to an object on the World Wide Web. URL is a constant object; after you create it, you can't change its fields. Many classes use a URL object, such as `URLConnection` and `HttpURLConnection`.

```
public final class URL implements java.io.Serializable
    transient URLStreamHandler handler;
    static URLStreamHandlerFactory factory;
    static Hashtable handlers;
    public boolean equals(Object obj)
    public final Object getContent() throws java.io.IOException
    public String getFile()
    public String getHost()
    public int getPort()
    public String getProtocol()
    public String getRef()
    static synchronized URLStreamHandler
        getURLStreamHandler(String protocol)
    public int hashCode()
    boolean hostsEqual(String h1, String h2)
    public URLConnection openConnection() throws
        java.io.IOException
    public final InputStream openStream() throws
        java.io.IOException
    public boolean sameFile(URL other)
    protected void set(String protocol, String host, int port,
        String file, String ref)
    public static synchronized void
        setURLStreamHandlerFactory(URLStreamHandlerFactory fac)
```

```
public String toExternalForm()
public String toString()
public URL(String protocol, String host, int port, String
    file) throws MalformedURLException
public URL(String protocol, String host, String file) throws
    MalformedURLException
public URL(String spec) throws MalformedURLException
public URL(URL context, String spec) throws
    MalformedURLException
```

java.net.URLConnection

URLConnection represents an active connection to an object represented by a URL. URLConnection is an abstract class, and so it can't be instantiated directly — don't even try it. You must either subclass it to implement a connection or obtain a URLConnection object by some other means. The URL class contains an openConnection() method that returns a URLConnection.

The HttpURLConnection class extends this class and provides additional functionality.

```
abstract public class URLConnection
    protected URL url;
    protected boolean doInput;
    protected boolean doOutput;
    protected boolean allowUserInteraction;
    protected boolean useCaches;
    protected long ifModifiedSince;
    public static FileNameMap fileNameMap;
    protected boolean connected;
    static ContentHandlerFactory factory;
    abstract public void connect() throws IOException;
    public boolean getAllowUserInteraction()
    public Object getContent() throws IOException
    public String getContentEncoding()
    synchronized ContentHandler getContentHandler() throws
        UnknownServiceException
    public int getContentLength()
    public String getContentType()
    public long getDate()
    public static boolean getDefaultAllowUserInteraction()
    public static String getDefaultRequestProperty(String key)
    public boolean getDefaultUseCaches()
    public boolean getDoInput()
    public boolean getDoOutput()
    public long getExpiration()
    public String getHeaderField(String name)
    public String getHeaderField(int n)
    public long getHeaderFieldDate(String name, long Default)
    public int getHeaderFieldInt(String name, int Default)
    public String getHeaderFieldKey(int n)
    public long getIfModifiedSince()
    public InputStream getInputStream() throws IOException
    public long getLastModified()
    public OutputStream getOutputStream() throws IOException
    public String getRequestProperty(String key)
```

(continued)

(continued)

```
public URL getURL()
public boolean getUseCaches()
protected static String guessContentTypeFromName(String
    fname)
static public String guessContentTypeFromStream(InputStream
    is) throws IOException
public void setAllowUserInteraction(boolean
    allowuserinteraction)
public static synchronized void
    setContentHandlerFactory(ContentHandlerFactory fac)
public static void setDefaultAllowUserInteraction(boolean
    defaultallowuserinteraction)
public static void setDefaultRequestProperty(String key,
    String value)
public void setDefaultUseCaches(boolean defaultusecaches)
public void setDoInput(boolean doinput)
public void setDoOutput(boolean dooutput)
public void setIfModifiedSince(long ifmodifiedsince)
public void setRequestProperty(String key, String value)
public void setUseCaches(boolean usecaches)
public String toString()
protected URLConnection(URL url)
```

java.net.URLEncoder

This class turns `Strings` of text into x-www-form-urlencoded format. The class contains only one method, `encode()`, that performs the encoding to be used when sending text on a `URL` string.

```
public class URLEncoder

    static BitSet dontNeedEncoding;
    public static String encode(String s)
```

java.net.URLStreamHandler

`URLStreamHandler` is an abstract class for `URL` stream openers. Subclasses of this class know how to create streams for particular protocol types. Most applications never need this class; don't be surprised if you never have the pleasure of calling on this class to do anything for you.

```
public abstract class URLStreamHandler

    abstract protected URLConnection openConnection(URL u)
        throws IOException;
    protected void parseURL(URL u, String spec, int start, int
        limit)
    protected void setURL(URL u, String protocol, String host,
        int port, String file, String ref)
    protected String toExternalForm(URL u)
```

java.net.URLStreamHandlerFactory

This interface defines a factory for `URLStreamHandler` instances. The `URL` class uses `URLStreamHandlerFactory` to create

URLStreamHandlers for various streams. You can probably just tuck this interface away in your memory banks — most applications don't use this interface.

```
public interface URLStreamHandlerFactory
    URLStreamHandler createURLStreamHandler(String protocol);
```

The java.sql Package

The creators of Java realized the power of using Java to access databases. To tap into that power, they developed a standard structured query language (SQL) database access interface called the JDBC (Java Database Connectivity) API. In Version 1.0 of the JDK, JDBC was a separate API and was not included in the JDK proper. JDBC is now a standard part of Java. The JDBC API allows programmers to access SQL databases using object-oriented, platform-independent Java code.

All the classes associated with the JDBC API are grouped together in the java.sql package. The following hierarchy diagram shows the relationship of all of the classes in the java.sql package:

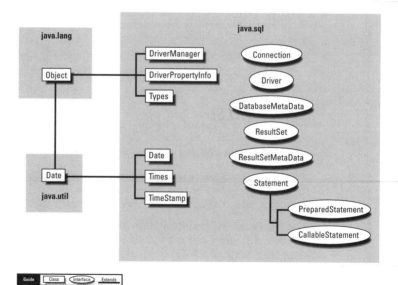

Using JDBC is not all that difficult. First you obtain a driver to supply the link between the JDBC driver manager and the underlying database (see "java.sql.DriverManager" in this section for more information). After you install the driver, you can get on with the Java programming! See "Using JDBC" in this section for the skinny on getting some real work done with JDBC.

java.sql.CallableStatement

JDBC provides a mechanism to call stored procedures (assuming your database supports stored procedures). This SQL syntax has one form that includes a result parameter and one that does not. If used, the result parameter must be registered as an OUT parameter. You can use other parameters for input, output, or both. Parameters are referred to sequentially starting from 1.

```
public interface CallableStatement extends PreparedStatement
    BigDecimal getBigDecimal(int parameterIndex, int scale)
        throws SQLException;
    boolean getBoolean(int parameterIndex) throws SQLException;
    byte getByte(int parameterIndex) throws SQLException;
    byte[] getBytes(int parameterIndex) throws SQLException;
    java.sql.Date getDate(int parameterIndex) throws
        SQLException;
    double getDouble(int parameterIndex) throws SQLException;
    float getFloat(int parameterIndex) throws SQLException;
    int getInt(int parameterIndex) throws SQLException;
    long getLong(int parameterIndex) throws SQLException;
    Object getObject(int parameterIndex) throws SQLException;
    short getShort(int parameterIndex) throws SQLException;
    String getString(int parameterIndex) throws SQLException;
    java.sql.Time getTime(int parameterIndex) throws
        SQLException;
    java.sql.Timestamp getTimestamp(int parameterIndex) throws
        SQLException;
    void registerOutParameter(int parameterIndex, int sqlType)
        throws SQLException;
    void registerOutParameter(int parameterIndex, int sqlType,
        int scale) throws SQLException;
    boolean wasNull() throws SQLException;
```

java.sql.Connection

Connection represents a session with a specific database. Basically, it gives you access to the database. With a Connection, SQL statements are executed and results are returned.

Connection provides information describing its tables, its supported SQL grammar, its stored procedures, its capabilities and more. You can obtain this information by using the getMetaData() method.

```
public interface Connection
    int TRANSACTION_NONE;
    int TRANSACTION_READ_UNCOMMITTED;
    int TRANSACTION_READ_COMMITTED;
    int TRANSACTION_REPEATABLE_READ;
    int TRANSACTION_SERIALIZABLE;
    void clearWarnings() throws SQLException;
    void close() throws SQLException;
```

```
void commit() throws SQLException;
Statement createStatement() throws SQLException;
boolean getAutoCommit() throws SQLException;
String getCatalog() throws SQLException;
DatabaseMetaData getMetaData() throws SQLException;
int getTransactionIsolation() throws SQLException;
SQLWarning getWarnings() throws SQLException;
boolean isClosed() throws SQLException;
boolean isReadOnly() throws SQLException;
String nativeSQL(String sql) throws SQLException;
CallableStatement prepareCall(String sql) throws
    SQLException;
PreparedStatement prepareStatement(String sql) throws
    SQLException;
void rollback() throws SQLException;
void setAutoCommit(boolean autoCommit) throws SQLException;
void setCatalog(String catalog) throws SQLException;
void setReadOnly(boolean readOnly) throws SQLException;
void setTransactionIsolation(int level) throws SQLException;
```

java.sql.DatabaseMetaData

DatabaseMetaData provides information about the database as a
whole. Many of the methods in this class return lists of information as ResultSets. You can use the normal ResultSet methods, such as getString() and getInt(), to retrieve the data
from these ResultSets. If a given form of metadata isn't available, these methods throw an SQLException.

```
public interface DatabaseMetaData
        int procedureResultUnknown;
        int procedureNoResult;
        int procedureReturnsResult;
        int procedureColumnUnknown;
        int procedureColumnIn;
        int procedureColumnInOut;
        int procedureColumnOut;
        int procedureColumnReturn;
        int procedureColumnResult;
        int procedureNoNulls;
        int procedureNullable;
        int procedureNullableUnknown;
        int columnNoNulls;
        int columnNullable;
        int columnNullableUnknown;
        int bestRowTemporary;
        int bestRowTransaction;
        int bestRowSession;
        int bestRowUnknown;
        int bestRowNotPseudo;
        int bestRowPseudo;
        int versionColumnUnknown;
        int versionColumnNotPseudo;
        int versionColumnPseudo;
        int typeNoNulls;
        int typeNullable;
        int typeNullableUnknown;
        int typePredNone;
        int typePredChar;
```

(continued)

(continued)

```
int typePredBasic;
int typeSearchable;
short tableIndexStatistic;
short tableIndexClustered;
short tableIndexHashed;
short tableIndexOther;
boolean allProceduresAreCallable() throws SQLException;
boolean allTablesAreSelectable() throws SQLException;
boolean dataDefinitionCausesTransactionCommit() throws
    SQLException;
boolean dataDefinitionIgnoredInTransactions() throws
    SQLException;
boolean doesMaxRowSizeIncludeBlobs() throws SQLException;
ResultSet getBestRowIdentifier(String catalog, String
    schema, String table, int scope, boolean nullable) throws
    SQLException;
ResultSet getCatalogs() throws SQLException;
String getCatalogSeparator() throws SQLException;
String getCatalogTerm() throws SQLException;
ResultSet getColumnPrivileges(String catalog, String schema,
    String table, String columnNamePattern) throws SQLException;
ResultSet getColumns(String catalog, String schemaPattern,
    String tableNamePattern, String columnNamePattern) throws
    SQLExceptiogetcolumns
String getDatabaseProductName() throws SQLException;
ResultSet getCrossReference( String primaryCatalog, String
    primarySchema, String primaryTable, String foreignCatalog,
    String forgetcrossreference
String getDatabaseProductVersion() throws SQLException;
int getDefaultTransactionIsolation() throws SQLException;
int getDriverMajorVersion();
int getDriverMinorVersion();
String getDriverName() throws SQLException;
String getDriverVersion() throws SQLException;
ResultSet getExportedKeys(String catalog, String schema,
    String table) throws SQLException;
String getExtraNameCharacters() throws SQLException;
String getIdentifierQuoteString() throws SQLException;
ResultSet getImportedKeys(String catalog, String schema,
    String table) throws SQLException;
ResultSet getIndexInfo(String catalog, String schema, String
    table, boolean unique, boolean approximate) throws
    SQLException;
int getMaxBinaryLiteralLength() throws SQLException;
int getMaxCatalogNameLength() throws SQLException;
int getMaxCharLiteralLength() throws SQLException;
int getMaxColumnNameLength() throws SQLException;
int getMaxColumnsInGroupBy() throws SQLException;
int getMaxColumnsInIndex() throws SQLException;
int getMaxColumnsInOrderBy() throws SQLException;
int getMaxColumnsInSelect() throws SQLException;
int getMaxColumnsInTable() throws SQLException;
int getMaxConnections() throws SQLException;
int getMaxCursorNameLength() throws SQLException;
int getMaxIndexLength() throws SQLException;
int getMaxProcedureNameLength() throws SQLException;
int getMaxRowSize() throws SQLException;
int getMaxSchemaNameLength() throws SQLException;
int getMaxStatementLength() throws SQLException;
int getMaxStatements() throws SQLException;
int getMaxTableNameLength() throws SQLException;
int getMaxTablesInSelect() throws SQLException;
int getMaxUserNameLength() throws SQLException;
```

```
String getNumericFunctions() throws SQLException;
ResultSet getPrimaryKeys(String catalog, String schema,
    String table) throws SQLException;
ResultSet getProcedureColumns(String catalog, String
    schemaPattern, String procedureNamePattern, String
    columnNamePattern) throwgetprocedurecolumns
ResultSet getProcedures(String catalog, String
    schemaPattern, String procedureNamePattern) throws
    SQLException;
String getProcedureTerm() throws SQLException;
ResultSet getSchemas() throws SQLException;
String getSchemaTerm() throws SQLException;
String getSearchStringEscape() throws SQLException;
String getSQLKeywords() throws SQLException;
String getStringFunctions() throws SQLException;
String getSystemFunctions() throws SQLException;
ResultSet getTablePrivileges(String catalog, String
    schemaPattern, String tableNamePattern) throws SQLException;
ResultSet getTables(String catalog, String schemaPattern,
    String tableNamePattern, String types[]) throws
    SQLException;
ResultSet getTableTypes() throws SQLException;
String getTimeDateFunctions() throws SQLException;
ResultSet getTypeInfo() throws SQLException;
String getURL() throws SQLException;
String getUserName() throws SQLException;
ResultSet getVersionColumns(String catalog, String schema,
    String table) throws SQLException;
boolean isCatalogAtStart() throws SQLException;
boolean isReadOnly() throws SQLException;
boolean nullPlusNonNullIsNull() throws SQLException;
boolean nullsAreSortedAtEnd() throws SQLException;
boolean nullsAreSortedAtStart() throws SQLException;
boolean nullsAreSortedHigh() throws SQLException;
boolean nullsAreSortedLow() throws SQLException;
boolean storesLowerCaseIdentifiers() throws SQLException;
boolean storesLowerCaseQuotedIdentifiers() throws
    SQLException;
boolean storesMixedCaseIdentifiers() throws SQLException;
boolean storesMixedCaseQuotedIdentifiers() throws
    SQLException;
boolean storesUpperCaseIdentifiers() throws SQLException;
boolean storesUpperCaseQuotedIdentifiers() throws
    SQLException;
boolean supportsAlterTableWithAddColumn() throws
    SQLException;
boolean supportsAlterTableWithDropColumn() throws
    SQLException;
boolean supportsANSI92EntryLevelSQL() throws SQLException;
boolean supportsANSI92FullSQL() throws SQLException;
boolean supportsANSI92IntermediateSQL() throws SQLException;
boolean supportsCatalogsInDataManipulation() throws
    SQLException;
boolean supportsCatalogsInIndexDefinitions() throws
    SQLException;
boolean supportsCatalogsInPrivilegeDefinitions() throws
    SQLException;
boolean supportsCatalogsInProcedureCalls() throws
    SQLException;
boolean supportsCatalogsInTableDefinitions() throws
    SQLException;
boolean supportsColumnAliasing() throws SQLException;
```

(continued)

(continued)
```
boolean supportsConvert() throws SQLException;
boolean supportsConvert(int fromType, int toType) throws
  SQLException;
boolean supportsCoreSQLGrammar() throws SQLException;
boolean supportsCorrelatedSubqueries() throws SQLException;
boolean supportsDataDefinitionAndDataManipulation
  Transactions() throws SQLException;
boolean supportsDataManipulationTransactionsOnly() throws
  SQLException;
boolean supportsDifferentTableCorrelationNames() throws
  SQLException;
boolean supportsExpressionsInOrderBy() throws SQLException;
boolean supportsExtendedSQLGrammar() throws SQLException;
boolean supportsFullOuterJoins() throws SQLException;
boolean supportsGroupBy() throws SQLException;
boolean supportsGroupByBeyondSelect() throws SQLException;
boolean supportsGroupByUnrelated() throws SQLException;
boolean supportsIntegrityEnhancementFacility() throws
  SQLException;
boolean supportsLikeEscapeClause() throws SQLException;
boolean supportsLimitedOuterJoins() throws SQLException;
boolean supportsMinimumSQLGrammar() throws SQLException;
boolean supportsMixedCaseIdentifiers() throws SQLException;
boolean supportsMixedCaseQuotedIdentifiers() throws
  SQLException;
boolean supportsMultipleResultSets() throws SQLException;
boolean supportsMultipleTransactions() throws SQLException;
boolean supportsNonNullableColumns() throws SQLException;
boolean supportsOpenCursorsAcrossCommit() throws
  SQLException;
boolean supportsOpenCursorsAcrossRollback() throws
  SQLException;
boolean supportsOpenStatementsAcrossCommit() throws
  SQLException;
boolean supportsOpenStatementsAcrossRollback() throws
  SQLException;
boolean supportsOrderByUnrelated() throws SQLException;
boolean supportsOuterJoins() throws SQLException;
boolean supportsPositionedDelete() throws SQLException;
boolean supportsPositionedUpdate() throws SQLException;
boolean supportsSchemasInDataManipulation() throws
  SQLException;
boolean supportsSchemasInIndexDefinitions() throws
  SQLException;
boolean supportsSchemasInPrivilegeDefinitions() throws
  SQLException;
boolean supportsSchemasInProcedureCalls() throws
  SQLException;
boolean supportsSchemasInTableDefinitions() throws
  SQLException;
boolean supportsSelectForUpdate() throws SQLException;
boolean supportsStoredProcedures() throws SQLException;
boolean supportsSubqueriesInComparisons() throws
  SQLException;
boolean supportsSubqueriesInExists() throws SQLException;
boolean supportsSubqueriesInIns() throws SQLException;
boolean supportsSubqueriesInQuantifieds() throws
  SQLException;
boolean supportsTableCorrelationNames() throws SQLException;
boolean supportsTransactionIsolationLevel(int level) throws
  SQLException;
```

```
boolean supportsTransactions() throws SQLException;
boolean supportsUnion() throws SQLException;
boolean supportsUnionAll() throws SQLException;
boolean usesLocalFilePerTable() throws SQLException;
boolean usesLocalFiles() throws SQLException;
```

java.sql.Date

This class is a thin wrapper around java.util.Date that allows JDBC to identify SQL DATE values. Date adds formatting and parsing operations to support the JDBC escape syntax for date values.

```
public class Date extends java.util.Date
    public Date(int year, int month, int day)
    public Date(long date)
    public int getHours()
    public int getMinutes()
    public int getSeconds()
    public void setHours(int i)
    public void setMinutes(int i)
    public void setSeconds(int i)
    public void setTime(long date)
    public String toString()
    public static Date valueOf(String s)
```

java.sql.Driver

The Java SQL framework allows the use of multiple database drivers. Each driver should supply a class that implements the Driver interface. The DriverManager loads as many drivers as it can find. For any given connection request, DriverManager asks each driver in turn to connect to the target URL.

We strongly recommend that you make each Driver class small and stand-alone so that the Driver class can be loaded and queried without bringing in vast quantities of supporting code.

When a Driver class is loaded, it should create an instance of itself and register it with the DriverManager. A user can load and register a driver by calling Class.forName("my.cool.Driver").

```
public interface Driver
    boolean acceptsURL(String url) throws SQLException;
    Connection connect(String url, java.util.Properties info)
        throws SQLException;
    int getMajorVersion();
    int getMinorVersion();
    DriverPropertyInfo[] getPropertyInfo(String url,
        java.util.Properties info) throws SQLException;
    boolean jdbcCompliant();
```

java.sql.DriverManager

DriverManager handles the connections to the underlying drivers, which actually supply the link to the database. These underlying drivers are usually supplied by third parties or database vendors. Three types of drivers are currently available: JDBC/ODBC bridge driver, JDBC net driver, and native JDBC driver.

As part of its initialization, DriverManager attempts to load all *known* drivers; that is, all drivers referenced in the jdbc.drivers system property. A user can customize the JDBC Drivers used by their applications. For example, in your ~/.hotjava/properties file you may specify: jdbc.drivers=my.cool.Driver: jdbc.my.Driver:jdbc.your.Driver. A program can also explicitly load JDBC drivers at any time. For example, the jdbc.odbc.Driver is loaded with the following statement:

```
Class.forName("jdbc.odbc.Driver");
```

The DriverManager class is a static object, meaning all methods are declared as static. That means you can't instantiate it directly, and you must envoke the methods by simply using the class name.

The following code provides an example of how to gain a connection to a database:

```
Connection myConn;  //myConn will store the connection
myConn = DriverManager.getConnection(Dbname, "user", "password");
```

After you establish the connection, you can then access the database with the connection object.

```
public class DriverManager
    public static void deregisterDriver(Driver driver) throws
        SQLException
    public static synchronized Connection getConnection(String
        url, java.util.Properties info) throws SQLException
    public static synchronized Connection getConnection(String
        url, String user, String password) throws SQLException
    public static synchronized Connection getConnection(String
        url) throws SQLException
    public static Driver getDriver(String url) throws
        SQLException
    public static java.util.Enumeration getDrivers()
    public static int getLoginTimeout()
    public static java.io.PrintStream getLogStream()
    static void initialize()
    public static void println(String message)
    public static synchronized void registerDriver
        (java.sql.Driver driver) throws SQLException
    public static void setLoginTimeout(int seconds)
    public static void setLogStream(java.io.PrintStream out)
```

java.sql.DriverPropertyInfo

Advanced programmers use DriverPropertyInfo to interact
with a Driver via getDriverProperties() to discover and
supply properties for connections.

```
public class DriverPropertyInfo
    public String name;
    public String description;
    public boolean required;
    public String value;
    public String[] choices;
    public DriverPropertyInfo(String name, String value)
```

java.sql.PreparedStatement

PreparedStatement allows an SQL statement to be pre-compiled
and stored in a PreparedStatement object. Doing so makes
execution more efficient, which you will appreciate if you need to
execute the statement multiple times.

The setXXX methods for setting IN parameter values must specify
types that are compatible with the defined SQL type of the input
parameter. For instance, if the IN parameter has SQL type Integer,
then setInt() should be used. If arbitrary parameter type
conversions are required, then the setObject() method should
be used with a target SQL type. See "java.sql.Types" in this section
for a mapping of SQL types to Java types.

```
public interface PreparedStatement extends Statement
    void clearParameters() throws SQLException;
    boolean execute() throws SQLException;
    ResultSet executeQuery() throws SQLException;
    int executeUpdate() throws SQLException;
    void setAsciiStream(int parameterIndex, java.io.InputStream
        x, int length) throws SQLException;
    void setBigDecimal(int parameterIndex, BigDecimal x) throws
        SQLException;
    void setBinaryStream(int parameterIndex, java.io.InputStream
        x, int length) throws SQLException;
    void setBoolean(int parameterIndex, boolean x) throws
        SQLException;
    void setByte(int parameterIndex, byte x) throws
        SQLException;
    void setBytes(int parameterIndex, byte x[]) throws
        SQLException;
    void setDate(int parameterIndex, java.sql.Date x) throws
        SQLException;
    void setDouble(int parameterIndex, double x) throws
        SQLException;
    void setFloat(int parameterIndex, float x) throws
        SQLException;
    void setInt(int parameterIndex, int x) throws SQLException;
    void setLong(int parameterIndex, long x) throws
        SQLException;
```

(continued)

(continued)

```
void setNull(int parameterIndex, int sqlType) throws
  SQLException;
void setObject(int parameterIndex, Object x, int
  targetSqlType, int scale) throws SQLException;
void setObject(int parameterIndex, Object x, int
  targetSqlType) throws SQLException;
void setObject(int parameterIndex, Object x) throws
  SQLException;
void setShort(int parameterIndex, short x) throws
  SQLException;
void setString(int parameterIndex, String x) throws
  SQLException;
void setTime(int parameterIndex, java.sql.Time x) throws
  SQLException;
void setTimestamp(int parameterIndex, java.sql.Timestamp x)
  throws SQLException;
void setUnicodeStream(int parameterIndex,
  java.io.InputStream x, int length) throws SQLException;
```

java.sql.ResultSet

A ResultSet provides access to a table of data generated by executing an SQL statement. The table rows are retrieved in sequence. Within a row, its column values can be accessed in any order. A ResultSet maintains a cursor pointing to its current row of data. The next() method moves the cursor to the next row. Initially, the cursor is positioned before the first row so the next() method must be called before the first row is read.

The getXXX (getByte(), getString(), getTime()) methods retrieve column values for the current row. You can retrieve values by either using the index number of the column or by using the name of the column, but the column index will be more efficient. Columns are numbered starting from 1. The getXXX methods cause the JDBC driver to attempt to convert the underlying data to the specified Java type and return a suitable Java value. See "java.sql.Types" in this section for a mapping of SQL types to Java types.

A ResultSet is automatically closed by the Statement that generates it when that Statement is closed, re-executed, or is used to retrieve the next result from a sequence of multiple results. The number, types, and properties of a ResultSet's columns are provided by the ResultSetMetaData object returned by the getMetaData() method.

```
public interface ResultSet

    void clearWarnings() throws SQLException;
    void close() throws SQLException;
    int findColumn(String columnName) throws SQLException;
    java.io.InputStream getAsciiStream(int columnIndex) throws
      SQLException;
    java.io.InputStream getAsciiStream(String columnName) throws
      SQLException;
```

```
BigDecimal getBigDecimal(int columnIndex, int scale) throws
    SQLException;
BigDecimal getBigDecimal(String columnName, int scale)
    throws SQLException;
java.io.InputStream getBinaryStream(int columnIndex) throws
    SQLException;
java.io.InputStream getBinaryStream(String columnName)
    throws SQLException;
boolean getBoolean(int columnIndex) throws SQLException;
boolean getBoolean(String columnName) throws SQLException;
byte getByte(int columnIndex) throws SQLException;
byte getByte(String columnName) throws SQLException;
byte[] getBytes(int columnIndex) throws SQLException;
byte[] getBytes(String columnName) throws SQLException;
String getCursorName() throws SQLException;
java.sql.Date getDate(int columnIndex) throws SQLException;
java.sql.Date getDate(String columnName) throws
    SQLException;
double getDouble(int columnIndex) throws SQLException;
double getDouble(String columnName) throws SQLException;
float getFloat(int columnIndex) throws SQLException;
float getFloat(String columnName) throws SQLException;
int getInt(int columnIndex) throws SQLException;
int getInt(String columnName) throws SQLException;
long getLong(int columnIndex) throws SQLException;
long getLong(String columnName) throws SQLException;
ResultSetMetaData getMetaData() throws SQLException;
Object getObject(int columnIndex) throws SQLException;
Object getObject(String columnName) throws SQLException;
short getShort(int columnIndex) throws SQLException;
short getShort(String columnName) throws SQLException;
String getString(int columnIndex) throws SQLException;
String getString(String columnName) throws SQLException;
java.sql.Time getTime(int columnIndex) throws SQLException;
java.sql.Time getTime(String columnName) throws
    SQLException;
java.sql.Timestamp getTimestamp(int columnIndex) throws
    SQLException;
java.sql.Timestamp getTimestamp(String columnName) throws
    SQLException;
java.io.InputStream getUnicodeStream(int columnIndex) throws
    SQLException;
java.io.InputStream getUnicodeStream(String columnName)
    throws SQLException;
SQLWarning getWarnings() throws SQLException;
boolean next() throws SQLException;
boolean wasNull() throws SQLException;
```

java.sql.ResultSetMetaData

A `ResultSetMetaData` object finds out about the types and
properties of the columns in a `ResultSet`. This is useful if you
don't know the details of a returned result set.
`ResultSetMetaData` contains many methods to help you find
out information about the result set. For example,
`getColumnCount()` returns the number of columns, and
`getColumnType()` takes the column number as an argument and
returns its data type.

```
public interface ResultSetMetaData
    int columnNoNulls;
    int columnNullable;
    int columnNullableUnknown;
    String getCatalogName(int column) throws SQLException;
    int getColumnCount() throws SQLException;
    int getColumnDisplaySize(int column) throws SQLException;
    String getColumnLabel(int column) throws SQLException;
    String getColumnName(int column) throws SQLException;
    int getColumnType(int column) throws SQLException;
    String getColumnTypeName(int column) throws SQLException;
    int getPrecision(int column) throws SQLException;
    int getScale(int column) throws SQLException;
    String getSchemaName(int column) throws SQLException;
    String getTableName(int column) throws SQLException;
    boolean isAutoIncrement(int column) throws SQLException;
    boolean isCaseSensitive(int column) throws SQLException;
    boolean isCurrency(int column) throws SQLException;
    boolean isDefinitelyWritable(int column) throws
        SQLException;
    int isNullable(int column) throws SQLException;
    boolean isReadOnly(int column) throws SQLException;
    boolean isSearchable(int column) throws SQLException;
    boolean isSigned(int column) throws SQLException;
    boolean isWritable(int column) throws SQLException;
```

java.sql.Statement

A Statement object executes a static SQL statement and obtains the results. The executeQuery() method executes the SQL statement and returns a ResultSet object.

Only one ResultSet per Statement can be open at one time. Therefore, if the reading of one ResultSet is interleaved with the reading of another, each must have been generated by different Statements. All statement-execute methods implicitly close a statement's current ResultSet if an open one exists.

```
public interface Statement
    void cancel() throws SQLException;
    void clearWarnings() throws SQLException;
    void close() throws SQLException;
    boolean execute(String sql) throws SQLException;
    ResultSet executeQuery(String sql) throws SQLException;
    int executeUpdate(String sql) throws SQLException;
    int getMaxFieldSize() throws SQLException;
    int getMaxRows() throws SQLException;
    boolean getMoreResults() throws SQLException;
    int getQueryTimeout() throws SQLException;
    ResultSet getResultSet() throws SQLException;
    int getUpdateCount() throws SQLException;
    SQLWarning getWarnings() throws SQLException;
    void setCursorName(String name) throws SQLException;
    void setEscapeProcessing(boolean enable) throws
        SQLException;
    void setMaxFieldSize(int max) throws SQLException;
    void setMaxRows(int max) throws SQLException;
    void setQueryTimeout(int seconds) throws SQLException;
```

java.sql.Time

This class is a thin wrapper around `java.util.Date` that allows JDBC to identify SQL TIME values. It adds formatting and parsing operations to support the JDBC escape syntax for time values.

```
public class Time extends java.util.Date
    public int getDate()
    public int getDay()
    public int getMonth()
    public int getYear()
    public void setDate(int i)
    public void setMonth(int i)
    public void setTime(long time)
    public void setYear(int i)
    public Time(int hour, int minute, int second)
    public Time(long time)
    public String toString()
    public static Time valueOf(String s)
```

java.sql.Timestamp

This class is a thin wrapper around `java.util.Date` that allows JDBC to identify SQL TIMESTAMP values. This class basically extends `java.util.Date` and adds a nanoseconds field.

```
public class Timestamp extends java.util.Date
    public boolean after(Timestamp ts)
    public boolean before(Timestamp ts)
    public boolean equals(Timestamp ts)
    public int getNanos()
    public void setNanos(int n)
    public Timestamp(int year, int month, int date, int hour,
        int minute, int second, int nano)
    public Timestamp(long time)
    public String toString()
    public static Timestamp valueOf(String s)
```

java.sql.Types

This class defines constants that are used to identify SQL types. The following table maps the SQL types to Java types:

SQL Type	Java Type
BIT	boolean
TINYINT	byte
SMALLINT	short
INTEGER	int
BIGINT	long
FLOAT	double

(continued)

SQL Type	Java Type
REAL	float
DOUBLE	double
NUMERIC	java.sql.Numeric
DECIMAL	java.sql.Numeric
CHAR	String
VARCHAR	String
LONGVARCHAR	String
DATE	java.sql.Date
TIME	java.sql.Time
TIMESTAMP	java.sql.Timestamp
BINARY	byte[]
VARBINARY	byte[]
LONGVARBINARY	byte[]

```
public class Types
    public final static int BIT;
    public final static int TINYINT;
    public final static int SMALLINT;
    public final static int INTEGER;
    public final static int BIGINT;
    public final static int FLOAT;
    public final static int REAL;
    public final static int DOUBLE;
    public final static int NUMERIC;
    public final static int DECIMAL;
    public final static int CHAR;
    public final static int VARCHAR;
    public final static int LONGVARCHAR;
    public final static int DATE;
    public final static int TIME;
    public final static int TIMESTAMP;
    public final static int BINARY;
    public final static int VARBINARY;
    public final static int LONGVARBINARY;
    public final static int NULL;
    public final static int OTHER;
```

Using JDBC

The following program uses the JDBC API to access a database. This example (called JDBCApp.java) demonstrates many aspects of the API, including obtaining a connection to a database, submitting a query, retrieving the result set from the query, and accessing metadata from the database.

We wrote this example on a Windows NT machine with the JDBC/ODBC bridge driver that comes with JDK 1.1. What a deal! We use Microsoft Access as the target database. However, the real power of this example is that you can use it to access any SQL database on any platform.

This program performs the following tasks:

+ Connects to the database

+ Obtains various metadata about the database and displays it in a text area

+ Obtains the name of all the columns from a specific table and displays it in a list box

+ Allows the user to click on the column of interest and then displays all the rows in that column in another text area

The following shows you the code for JDBCApp.java:

```java
import java.awt.*;
import java.awt.event.*;
import java.util.*;
import java.sql.*;

class JDBCApp extends Frame {
List columnList;
TextArea resultList;
TextArea metaDataList;
ResultSet myResults;
Statement myStmt;
Connection myConnection;
String results[][];

public JDBCApp () {
super("Cool Database Demo");
this.setLayout(new BorderLayout());
Panel titlePanel = new Panel();
titlePanel.setLayout(new GridLayout(1,3));
Panel dataPanel = new Panel();
dataPanel.setLayout(new GridLayout(1,3));
add("North", titlePanel);
add("Center", dataPanel);
columnList = new List();
resultList = new TextArea();
metaDataList = new TextArea();
resultList.setEditable(false);
metaDataList.setEditable(false);

titlePanel.add(new Label("Database info",Label.CENTER));
titlePanel.add(new Label("Column info",Label.CENTER));
titlePanel.add(new Label("Column Data",Label.CENTER));
dataPanel.add(metaDataList);
dataPanel.add(columnList);
dataPanel.add(resultList);
initConnection();
columnList.addActionListener(new ListLis());
addWindowListener(new WindowLis());
}

public void initConnection() {
```

(continued)

(continued)

```
try {
    // Load Bridge Driver
    Class.forName ("sun.jdbc.odbc.JdbcOdbcDriver");
    // Establish connection to database
    // with DSN=wilma, user=sa, and no password
    myConnection = DriverManager.getConnection
    ("jdbc:odbc:wilma","sa","");
    // Create a statement object
    myStmt = myConnection.createStatement();
    // Execute statement
    myResults = myStmt.executeQuery("select * from Events");
    // Obtain meta data result set
    ResultSetMetaData myInfo = myResults.getMetaData();
    // Obtain database meta data
    DatabaseMetaData myInfo2 = myConnection.getMetaData();
    // Add driver name, driver version, and database product to
    text area
    metaDataList.append(myInfo2.getDriverName()+"\n");
    metaDataList.append(myInfo2.getDriverVersion()+"\n");
    metaDataList.append(myInfo2.getDatabaseProductName()+"\n");
    // Add column names to List.
    int colcount = myInfo.getColumnCount();
    for (int i = 1; i <= colcount; i++) {
        columnList.addItem(myInfo.getColumnName(i));
    }
    } catch (SQLException ex){
        System.out.println("SQLEXCEPTION");
    } catch (ClassNotFoundException ex){
    }
}
/**
 * Method used to query the data from database and display the
   appropriate
 * column data in the text area.
 */
public void getData(int i){
try {
    myResults = myStmt.executeQuery("select * from Events");
    while (myResults.next()){
        resultList.append(myResults.getString(i+1)+"\n");
    }
} catch (SQLException ex){
    System.out.println("Error in getData");
    }
}

class WindowLis extends WindowAdapter {
public void windowClosing(WindowEvent e){
    System.exit(0);
    }
}

class ListLis implements ActionListener {
public void actionPerformed(ActionEvent e) {
    int i = columnList.getSelectedIndex();
    resultList.setText("");
    getData(i);
    }
}
```

```
public static void main(String ar[]){
JDBCApp as = new JDBCApp();
as.setSize(500,200);
as.show();
}
}
```

The JDBCApp constructor method sets up two text areas and a list box to display the results.

The initConnection() method performs most of the good stuff. The class.forName() method loads a driver. (We load the JDBC/ODBC bridge driver that comes with JDK 1.1.) We then use DriverManager.getConnection() to obtain a connection object for our database. After we have a connection object, we use that to create a statement object with createStatement. The SQL statement is then sent to the database with the executeQuery() method and the results are captured in a ResultSet object.

Next, we obtain information about the result set returned (such as column names), and about the database itself (such as the driver). This information is known as *metadata*. ResultSetMetaData objects access information about result sets. This object is obtained by evoking the getMetaData() method on the result set. DatabaseMetaData stores information about the database. You obtain DatabaseMetaData by calling the getMetaData() method on the Connection object.

After the metadata objects are created, they can be interrogated with any of the methods available in the respective classes. In this example, we use getDriverName(), getDriverVersion(), and getDatabaseProductName() on the DatabaseMetaData object. The number of columns and column names are retrieved from ResultSetMetaData and are added to the list box.

The rest of the program allows the user to double-click on a column name in the list box and have all the fields from that column appear in the text area on the right. The inner class ListLis handles the user double-click events in the list box. The index of the item chosen in the list box is obtained and passed to the getData() method, which uses the new event model of JDK 1.1.

The getData() method queries the database and displays the proper column data. The result set returned is accessed with the getString() method because all of our data was stored as strings. The getXXX methods of ResultSet take a column identifier argument. This argument is either the column name or number starting from 1. To move the result set pointer to the next row, the next() method must be called.

TIP

When a result set is first returned, the pointer appears before the first row. The `next()` method must be called before you can even access the first row. If you always access the result set in a `while` loop, you can rest assured that things will go as planned.

The following figure shows you the results of all this beautiful code:

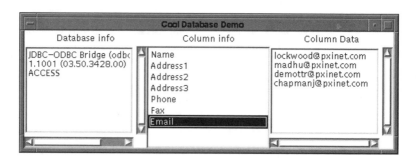

The java.util Package

The "utility" classes in this package provide all kinds of services for the rest of the language. For example, if you need classes to create data structures (such as hashtables), look no further. If you are interested in the date, this package offers a `Date` class as well as a `Calendar` class that you may find very helpful.

The `java.util` package also contains many tools to "internationalize" your Java programs in a snap. The world-wide reach of the Internet demands global software that can be developed independently of the nationality or language of its users. Java inherently provides internationalization by supporting the Unicode character. (The Unicode character set is the 16-bit superset of ASCII that allows the use of international characters.)

Now that we have you so excited about working with this package, take a gander at the class hierarchy for `java.util`:

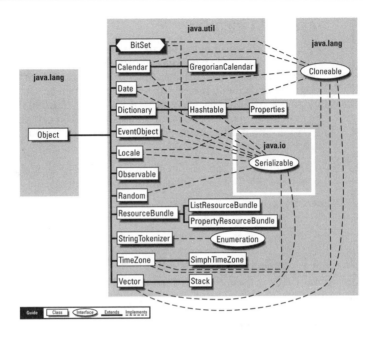

java.util.BitSet

BitSet operates on an arbitrary set of bits and is used to manipulate the state of each bit. What is manipulating the state of each bit? Simple: Being able to set the bit to 1, clear the bit to 0, get the value of the bit, and perform various boolean operations.

BitSet performs all of the functions you would expect, such as get(), set(), clear(), and(), and or(), that query, set, clear, and perform bitwise boolean arithmetic on the bits.

```
public final class BitSet implements Cloneable,
java.io.Serializable
    final static int BITS;
    final static int MASK;
    long bits[];
    public void and(BitSet set)
    public BitSet()
    public BitSet(int nbits)
    public void clear(int bit)
    public Object clone()
    public boolean equals(Object obj)
    public boolean get(int bit)
    public int hashCode()
    public void or(BitSet set)
    public void set(int bit)
    public int size()
    public String toString()
    public void xor(BitSet set)
```

java.util.Calendar

Calendar converts between a Date object and a particular
calender. A Calendar object can produce all the time field values
needed to implement the date-time formatting for a particular
language and calendar style (for example, Japanese -Gregorian,
Japanese-Traditional). Calendar is abstract, meaning that it must
be subclassed in order to create an instance. You can also use
Calendar to define GregorianCalendar (see "java.util.
GregorianCalendar" in this part).

A Date object defines a specific time with milliseconds precision.
(See "java.util.Date" in this part for more details.)

```
public abstract class Calendar implements Serializable, Cloneable
    public final static int ERA;
    public final static int YEAR;
    public final static int MONTH;
    public final static int WEEKOFYEAR;
    public final static int WEEKOFMONTH;
    public final static int DATE;
    public final static int DAYOFMONTH;
    public final static int DAYOFYEAR;
    public final static int DAYOFWEEK;
    public final static int DAYOFWEEKINMONTH;
    public final static int AMPM;
    public final static int HOUR;
    public final static int HOUROFDAY;
    public final static int MINUTE;
    public final static int SECOND;
    public final static int MILLISECOND;
    public final static int ZONEOFFSET;
    public final static int DSTOFFSET;
    public final static int FIELDCOUNT;
    public final static int SUNDAY;
    public final static int MONDAY;
    public final static int TUESDAY;
    public final static int WEDNESDAY;
    public final static int THURSDAY;
    public final static int FRIDAY;
    public final static int SATURDAY;
    public final static int JANUARY;
    public final static int FEBRUARY;
    public final static int MARCH;
    public final static int APRIL;
    public final static int MAY;
    public final static int JUNE;
    public final static int JULY;
    public final static int AUGUST;
    public final static int SEPTEMBER;
    public final static int OCTOBER;
    public final static int NOVEMBER;
    public final static int DECEMBER;
    public final static int UNDECIMBER;
    public final static int AM;
    public final static int PM;
    protected int fields[];
    protected boolean isSet[];
    protected long time;
```

```
protected boolean isTimeSet;
protected boolean areFieldsSet;
abstract public void add(int field, int amount) throws
    IllegalArgumentException;
abstract public boolean after(Object when);
abstract public boolean before(Object when);
protected Calendar()
protected Calendar(TimeZone zone, Locale aLocale)
public final void clear()
public final void clear(int field) throws
    IllegalArgumentException
public Object clone()
protected void complete() throws IllegalArgumentException
protected abstract void computeFields();
protected abstract void computeTime();
abstract public boolean equals(Object when);
public final int get(int field) throws
    IllegalArgumentException
public static synchronized Locale[] getAvailableLocales()
public static synchronized Calendar getInstance()
public static synchronized Calendar getInstance(TimeZone
    zone)
public static synchronized Calendar getInstance(Locale
    aLocale)
public static synchronized Calendar getInstance(TimeZone
    zone, Locale aLocale)
public int getFirstDayOfWeek()
abstract public int getGreatestMinimum(int field);
abstract public int getLeastMaximum(int field);
abstract public int getMaximum(int field);
public int getMinimalDaysInFirstWeek()
abstract public int getMinimum(int field);
public final Date getTime()
protected long getTimeInMillis()
public TimeZone getTimeZone()
public boolean isLenient()
protected final int internalGet(int field) throws
    IllegalArgumentException
public final boolean isSet(int field) throws
    IllegalArgumentException
abstract public void roll(int field, boolean up) throws
    IllegalArgumentException;
public final void set(int field, int value) throws
    IllegalArgumentException
public final void set(int year, int month, int date)
public final void set(int year, int month, int date, int
    hour, int minute)
public final void set(int year, int month, int date, int
    hour, int minute, int second)
public void setFirstDayOfWeek(int value)
public void setMinimalDaysInFirstWeek(int value)
public final void setTime(Date date)
protected void setTimeInMillis( long millis )
public void setTimeZone(TimeZone value)
public void setLenient(boolean mode)
```

java.util.Date

This class represents an instant in time with millisecond precision.
Many of the methods in this class in versions of the JDK prior to
1.1 are deprecated in order to support internationalization.

Deprecated methods maintain backward compatability, but you shouldn't use them in current implementations. Deprecated methods are mostly format conversions now supported in the `Calendar` and `DateFormat` classes.

If you're using a version of the JDK prior to 1.1, you may note that `Date` has problems handling dates before January 1, 1970. This could be a serious problem for anyone born before 1970, because Java could not compute how old you are — actually, this could be good if you're trying to evade any extra candles on your birthday cake.

In the 1.1 Version of the JDK, you should only use two of the constructors to create a `Date` object: the `no` argument and the `long` argument. The `no` argument constructor creates a `Date` object containing the current date; the `long` argument creates a `Date` object given the number of milliseconds from the epoch (January 1, 1970). Negative values represent dates before the epoch. All other constructors are deprecated.

```
public class Date implements java.io.Serializable, Cloneable
    public boolean after(Date when)
    public boolean before(Date when)
    public Date()
    public Date(long date)
    public Date(int year, int month, int date)
    public Date(int year, int month, int date, int hrs, int min)
    public Date(int year, int month, int date, int hrs, int min,
        int sec)
    public Date(String s)
    public boolean equals(Object obj)
    public int getDate()
    public int getDay()
    public int getHours()
    public int getMinutes()
    public int getMonth()
    public int getSeconds()
    public long getTime()
    public int getTimezoneOffset()
    public int getYear()
    public int hashCode()
    public static long parse(String s)
    public void setDate(int date)
    public void setHours(int hours)
    public void setMinutes(int minutes)
    public void setMonth(int month)
    public void setSeconds(int seconds)
    public void setTime(long time)
    public void setYear(int year)
    public String toGMTString()
    public String toLocaleString()
    public String toString()
    public static long UTC(int year, int month, int date, int
        hrs, int min, int sec)
    private void writeObject(ObjectOutputStream s) throws
        IOException
```

java.util.Dictionary

Dictionary is an abstract class used by HashTable and Properties. The main methods are put() and get().

```
public abstract class Dictionary
    abstract public Enumeration elements();
    abstract public Object get(Object key);
    abstract public boolean isEmpty();
    abstract public Enumeration keys();
    abstract public Object put(Object key, Object value);
    abstract public Object remove(Object key);
    abstract public int size();
```

java.util.Enumeration

Enumeration defines two methods used by other classes in this package. These two methods offer a variety of services to the other classes in this package. For example, you can use this interface to create a linked list. Many of the data structures provided, such as a Hashtable, also have methods that return an Enumeration object.

To use an Enumeration object, call hasMoreElements() within a loop. This method returns true if any elements remain in the list. The nextElement() method returns an object of type Object, which is the next element in the list.

```
public interface Enumeration
    boolean hasMoreElements();
    Object nextElement();
```

java.util.EventListener

All event listener interfaces must extend this tagging interface. Period. End of story. No discussion.

```
public interface EventListener
```

java.util.EventObject

You won't do much with this class, but here it is, just in case you run across one of these methods somewhere.

```
public class EventObject implements java.io.Serializable
    protected transient Object source;
    public EventObject(Object source)
    public Object getSource()
    public String toString()
```

java.util.GregorianCalendar

This class represents the Gregorian calendar, which is the calendar that most (but not all) of the world uses. The Date class allows the creation of Date objects given milliseconds from the epoch (January 1, 1970). You should use the GregorianCalendar class when creating a Date given anything other than milliseconds from the epoch. The Calendar subclasses provide additional internationalization.

```
public class GregorianCalendar extends Calendar
    public static final int AD;
    public static final int BC;
    public void add(int field, int amount) throws
        IllegalArgumentException
    public boolean after(Object when)
    public boolean before(Object when)
    public Object clone()
    protected void computeFields()
    protected void computeTime()
    public boolean equals(Object obj)
    public int getGreatestMinimum(int field)
    public final Date getGregorianChange()
    public int getLeastMaximum(int field)
    public int getMaximum(int field)
    public int getMinimum(int field)
    public GregorianCalendar()
    public GregorianCalendar(TimeZone zone)
    public GregorianCalendar(Locale aLocale)
    public GregorianCalendar(TimeZone zone, Locale aLocale)
    public GregorianCalendar(int year, int month, int date)
    public GregorianCalendar(int year, int month, int date, int
        hour, int minute)
    public GregorianCalendar(int year, int month, int date, int
        hour, int minute, int second)
    public synchronized int hashCode()
    public boolean isLeapYear(int year)
    public void roll(int field, boolean up) throws
        IllegalArgumentException
    public void setGregorianChange(Date date)
```

java.util.Hashtable

Are you interested in holding key/value pairs? If so, this class is for you. This class creates a hashtable data structure that stores objects (values) with non-numeric indicies (keys). This allows you to retrieve the value knowing the key.

Keys and values can be of any object type, but keys are typically Strings. The typical methods, such as get() and put(), are defined. keys() and elements() return Enumeration objects that can be used to iterate through the entire table.

```
public class Hashtable extends Dictionary implements Cloneable,
java.io.Serializable
    public synchronized void clear()
    public synchronized Object clone()
```

```
public synchronized boolean contains(Object value)
public synchronized boolean containsKey(Object key)
public synchronized Enumeration elements()
public synchronized Object get(Object key)
public Hashtable(int initialCapacity, float loadFactor)
public Hashtable(int initialCapacity)
public Hashtable()
public boolean isEmpty()
public synchronized Enumeration keys()
public synchronized Object put(Object key, Object value)
protected void rehash()
public synchronized Object remove(Object key)
public int size()
public synchronized String toString()
```

java.util.ListResourceBundle

This abstract class represents resources for a locale. When you subclass this class, you need to override getContents() and supply an array where each item in the array is a pair of objects. The first element of each pair is a String key, and the second is the value associated with that key.

```
public abstract class ListResourceBundle extends ResourceBundle
    abstract protected Object[][] getContents();
    public Enumeration getKeys()
    public final Object handleGetObject(String key)
```

java.util.Locale

This class contains information to support internationalization. Locale is declared final — don't think about subclassing it and changing the world.

In the Java international architecture, a *locale* is the mechanism for identifying the kind of object (NumberFormat, for example) that you would like to get. The locale is just a mechanism for identifying objects, not a container for the objects themselves. The country-specific language and behavior for these objects can then be added later independent of the code.

```
public final class Locale implements Cloneable, Serializable
    static public final Locale ENGLISH;
    static public final Locale FRENCH;
    static public final Locale GERMAN;
    static public final Locale ITALIAN;
    static public final Locale JAPANESE;
    static public final Locale KOREAN;
    static public final Locale CHINESE;
    static public final Locale SIMPLIFIED_CHINESE;
    static public final Locale TRADITIONAL_CHINESE;
    static public final Locale FRANCE;
    static public final Locale GERMANY;
    static public final Locale ITALY;
    static public final Locale JAPAN;
```

(continued)

(continued)

```
static public final Locale KOREA;
static public final Locale CHINA;
static public final Locale PRC;
static public final Locale TAIWAN;
static public final Locale UK;
static public final Locale US;
static public final Locale CANADA;
static public final Locale CANADA_FRENCH;
public Object clone()
public boolean equals(Object obj)
public String getCountry()
public static synchronized Locale getDefault()
public final String getDisplayCountry()
public String getDisplayCountry(Locale inLocale)
public final String getDisplayLanguage()
public String getDisplayLanguage(Locale inLocale)
public final String getDisplayName()
public String getDisplayName(Locale inLocale)
public final String getDisplayVariant()
public String getDisplayVariant(Locale inLocale)
public String getISO3Country() throws
  MissingResourceException
public String getISO3Language() throws
  MissingResourceException
public String getLanguage()
public String getVariant()
public synchronized int hashCode()
public Locale(String language, String country, String
  variant)
public Locale(String language, String country)
public static synchronized void setDefault(Locale newLocale)
public final String toString()
```

java.util.Observable

Observable, which works in conjunction with the Observer
class, allows different classes to notify each other of changes.

To use this class, create an instance and invoke addObserver()
with an instance of a class that implements Observer. When you
invoke notifyObservers(), the update() methods of all of the
classes you add are invoked.

```
public class Observable
    public synchronized void addObserver(Observer o)
    protected synchronized void clearChanged()
    public synchronized int countObservers()
    public synchronized void deleteObserver(Observer o)
    public synchronized void deleteObservers()
    public synchronized boolean hasChanged()
    public void notifyObservers()
    public void notifyObservers(Object arg)
    public Observable()
    protected synchronized void setChanged()
```

java.util.Observer

You use this interface in conjunction with the Observable class. Classes interested in being notified of a change from an Observable class should implement this interface and fill in the update() method. This update() method is automatically called when the object being observed notifies its observers.

```
public interface Observer
    void update(Observable o, Object arg);
```

java.util.Properties

Properties is a type of Hashtable that can be stored or retrieved from a stream. See "java.util.Hashtable" in this part.

```
public class Properties extends Hashtable
    protected Properties defaults;
    public String getProperty(String key)
    public String getProperty(String key, String defaultValue)
    public void list(PrintStream out)
    public void list(PrintWriter out)
    public synchronized void load(InputStream in) throws
        IOException
    public Properties()
    public Properties(Properties defaults)
    public Enumeration propertyNames()
    public synchronized void save(OutputStream out, String
        header)
```

java.util.PropertyResourceBundle

PropertyResourceBundle is subclassed from ResourceBundle to allow resources to be loaded from a property file. To create the file, create a property file with the keys (and their values) that you use in your source code in calls to ResourceBundle.getString(), and so on.

See "java.util.ResourceBundle" in this part for more information on ResourceBundles.

```
public class PropertyResourceBundle extends ResourceBundle
    public Enumeration getKeys()
    public Object handleGetObject(String key)
    public PropertyResourceBundle(InputStream stream) throws
        IOException
```

java.util.Random

Random is really pseudo random, of course (deterministic machines have a hard time generating real random numbers). Random resembles the random() method in the Math class, but you get more stuff, including the nextGaussian() method, which returns a double with Gaussian distribution and standard deviation 1.0. You can also set the seed, as well.

```
public class Random implements java.io.Serializable
    synchronized protected int next(int bits)
    public void nextBytes(byte[] bytes)
    public double nextDouble()
    public float nextFloat()
    synchronized public double nextGaussian()
    public int nextInt()
    public long nextLong()
    public Random()
    public Random(long seed)
    synchronized public void setSeed(long seed)
```

java.util.ResourceBundle

The programs produced with ResourceBundle can be localized or translated into different languages, which means added audience for your applications. A single program using ResourceBundles can provide multiple resources for different languages. Instead of using "hard-coded" strings as your button labels, choice lists, and so on, you write your code to load them out of a ResourceBundle. The text string is loaded by requesting the value associated with a certain key. The key is anything you want and is used in your code in calls to ResourceBundle, getString, and so on, to access that value. You can also add resources later without modifying your source code.

ResourceBundle is an abstract class and can't be instantiated directly. The class contains a static method getResourceBundle() that returns a ResourceBundle object. See PropertyResoure Bundle as a way to store resources in a property file.

```
abstract public class ResourceBundle
    static StackLookup stackLookup;
    static SystemClassLoader systemClassLoader;
    protected ResourceBundle parent;
    StringBuffer localeName, ClassLoader loader, boolean
        includeBase)
    public abstract Enumeration getKeys();
    public final Menu getMenu(String key) throws
        MissingResourceException
    public final MenuBar getMenuBar(String key) throws
        MissingResourceException
    public final Object getObject(String key) throws
        MissingResourceException
    public static final ResourceBundle getBundle(String
        baseName) throws MissingResourceException
    public static final ResourceBundle getBundle(String
        baseName, Locale locale)
    public final String getString(String key) throws
        MissingResourceException
    public final String[] getStringArray(String key) throws
        MissingResourceException
```

```
protected abstract Object handleGetObject(String key) throws
   MissingResourceException;
static class StackLookup extends java.lang.SecurityManager
   protected void setParent( ResourceBundle parent )
```

java.util.SimpleTimeZone

Use this class to create your own time zone for use with a
Gregorian calendar.

This simple class doesn't handle historical changes. The
dayOfWeekInMonth can be negative to mean from the end of the
month backwards. For example, Daylight Savings Time ends at the
last (-1) Sunday in October, at 2:00 a.m. in Standard Time.

```
public class SimpleTimeZone extends TimeZone

   public Object clone()
   public boolean equals(Object obj)
   public int getOffset(int era, int year, int month, int day,
      int dayOfWeek, int millis)
   public int getRawOffset()
   public synchronized int hashCode()
   public boolean inDaylightTime(Date date)
   public void setEndRule(int month, int dayOfWeekInMonth, int
      dayOfWeek, int time)
   public void setRawOffset(int offsetMillis)
   public void setStartRule(int month, int dayOfWeekInMonth,
      int dayOfWeek, int time)
   public void setStartYear(int year)
   public SimpleTimeZone(int rawOffset, String ID)
   public SimpleTimeZone(int rawOffset, String ID, int
      startMonth, int startDayOfWeekInMonth, int startDayOfWeek,
      int startTime, insimpletimezone
   public boolean useDaylightTime()
```

java.util.Stack

This class may seem familiar — you probably studied (or didn't
study) this classic last-in, first-out data structure in the second
computer science course you ever took. Using Stack, you can
store any type of object you want. You don't have to worry about
size, because Stack extends Vector, which is more or less a
growable array.

The Stack class is very useful when implementing a reverse
polish notation (RPN) calculator. The Stack class can be used for
the calculator's stack.

```
public class Stack extends Vector

   public boolean empty()
   public synchronized Object peek()
   public synchronized Object pop()
   public Object push(Object item)
   public synchronized int search(Object o)
```

java.util.StringTokenizer

The StringTokenizer class comes in handy when splitting strings. You can specify the characters to break on; if you don't specify particular characters, white space is assumed. This class breaks your string each time it encounters a token. The hasMoreElements() and nextToken() methods obtain the tokens in order. After you obtain all your tokens, insert them into your favorite video game machine.

```
public class StringTokenizer implements Enumeration
    public int countTokens()
    public boolean hasMoreElements()
    public boolean hasMoreTokens()
    public Object nextElement()
    public String nextToken()
    public String nextToken(String delim)
    public StringTokenizer(String str, String delim, boolean
        returnTokens)
    public StringTokenizer(String str, String delim)
    public StringTokenizer(String str)
```

java.util.TimeZone

TimeZone assists with internationalization by allowing you to specify your time zone with respect to the time in Greenwich (UTC). To create a time zone, use the getTimeZone() method along with a given time zone ID (EST is the ID for Eastern Standard Time, for example).

TIP The getAvailableIDs() method returns an array of all available IDs. The getDefault() method returns the current time zone where you live.

```
abstract public class TimeZone implements Serializable, Cloneable
    public Object clone()
    public static synchronized String[] getAvailableIDs(int
        rawOffset)
    public static synchronized String[] getAvailableIDs()
    public static synchronized TimeZone getDefault()
    public String getID()
    abstract public int getOffset(int era, int year, int month,
        int day, int dayOfWeek, int milliseconds);
    abstract public int getRawOffset();
    public static synchronized TimeZone getTimeZone(String ID)
    abstract public boolean inDaylightTime(Date date)
    public static synchronized void setDefault(TimeZone zone)
    public void setID(String ID)
    abstract public void setRawOffset(int offsetMillis);
    static
    abstract public boolean useDaylightTime();
```

java.util.Vector

Vector is a dynamically growable array. You should use the constructor that accepts the initial size and increment values.

WARNING!

Try to make an educated guess on the typical starting size and increment. If you don't, the vector may be less efficient.

```
public class Vector implements Cloneable, java.io.Serializable
    protected Object elementData[];
    protected int elementCount;
    protected int capacityIncrement;
    public final synchronized void addElement(Object obj)
    public final int capacity()
    public synchronized Object clone()
    public final boolean contains(Object elem)
    public final synchronized void copyInto(Object anArray[])
    public final synchronized Object elementAt(int index)
    public final synchronized Enumeration elements()
    public final synchronized void ensureCapacity(int
      minCapacity)
    public final synchronized Object firstElement()
    public final int indexOf(Object elem)
    public final synchronized int indexOf(Object elem, int
      index)
    public final synchronized void insertElementAt(Object obj,
      int index)
    public final boolean isEmpty()
    public final synchronized Object lastElement()
    public final int lastIndexOf(Object elem)
    public final synchronized int lastIndexOf(Object elem, int
      index)
    public final synchronized void removeAllElements()
    public final synchronized boolean removeElement(Object obj)
    public final synchronized void removeElementAt(int index)
    public final synchronized void setElementAt(Object obj, int
      index)
    public final synchronized void setSize(int newSize)
    public final int size()
    public final synchronized String toString()
    public final synchronized void trimToSize()
    public Vector(int initialCapacity, int capacityIncrement)
    public Vector(int initialCapacity)
    public Vector()
```

The java.util.zip Package

Sometimes we can't help picking favorites. We just have to tell you that java.util.zip is a very cool package.

We all seem to suffer from a lack of storage space from time to time. That's why we thank our lucky stars for file compression utilities, such as ZIP or GZIP. Think how great it would be if you had several classes that would compress data for you. Well guess what? That's right — the classes in this package are built especially for compressing and decompressing data in ZIP and GZIP formats.

The following figure shows the class hierarchy of the java.util.zip package, our personal vote for Package of the Year:

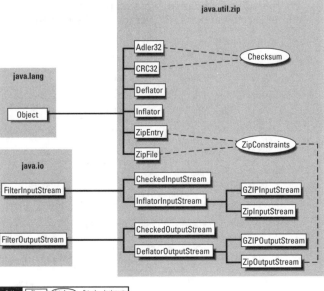

java.util.zip

Adler32 --- Checksum
CRC32 ---
Deflator
Inflator
ZipEntry --- ZipConstraints
ZipFile ---

java.lang

Object

java.io

FilterInputStream

CheckedInputStream
InflatorInputStream
GZIPInputStream
ZipInputStream

FilterOutputStream

CheckedOutputStream
DeflatorOutputStream
GZIPOutputStream
ZipOutputStream

Guide Class Interface Extends Implements

java.util.zip.Adler32

This class computes *checksums* using the Adler-32 algorithm.
Checksums help your computer verify that information coming
through its modem (or any other communication channel) has
been received properly.

Adler32 is almost as good as CRC32 (another error-detection
technique) in computing checksums and is much faster. The class
is a breeze to use; just create an instance and invoke either of the
update methods with your data. You can call `reset()` to start
over if you need to.

This class implements `Checksum`; you can use it with other
classes in this package.

```
public class Adler32 implements Checksum
    public native void update(byte[] b, int off, int len);
    public long getValue()
    public void reset()
    public void update(int b)
```

java.util.zip.CRC32

This class computes checksums using the CRC32 algorithm
and is almost identical to the `Adler32` class. The class is easy to
use — just create an instance and invoke either of the update

methods with your data. You can call reset( ) to start over, if the need arises.

This class implements Checksum, so you can use it with other classes in this package.

```
public class CRC32 implements Checksum
    public native void update(byte[] b, int off, int len);
    public long getValue()
    public void reset()
    public void update(int b)
```

java.util.zip.CheckedInputStream

This FilterInputStream computes a checksum of a stream. You can specify the algorithm used to compute the checksum as an argument to the constructor.

```
public class CheckedInputStream extends FilterInputStream
    public CheckedInputStream(InputStream in, Checksum cksum)
    public Checksum getChecksum()
    public int read() throws IOException
    public int read(byte[] buf, int off, int len) throws
        IOException
    public long skip(long n) throws IOException
```

java.util.zip.CheckedOutputStream

This FilterOutputStream computes a checksum of a stream. You can specify the algorithm used to compute the checksum as an argument to the constructor.

```
public class CheckedOutputStream extends FilterOutputStream
    public CheckedOutputStream(OutputStream out, Checksum cksum)
    public Checksum getChecksum()
    public void write(int b) throws IOException
    public void write(byte[] b, int off, int len) throws
        IOException
```

java.util.zip.Checksum

This interface defines the methods of a checksum class. Other classes in this package, such as the Adler32 and CRC32 classes, use Checksum.

Remember: Refer to the class hierarchy diagram at the beginning of this section for a concise representation of the relationship of all classes and interfaces in this package.

```
public interface Checksum
    public void update(int b);
    public void update(byte[] b, int off, int len);
    public long getValue();
    public void reset();
```

java.util.zip.Deflater

Some classes just take the wind out of you. Deflater does the same thing to your byte arrays by taking a compressed byte array and making it into an uncompressed byte array. Deflater uses the ZLIB compression library to decompress, therefore it must have been originally compressed using ZLIB. See "java.util. zip.Inflater" in this part for methods to compress a byte array using ZLIB.

```
public class Deflater
    public static final int DEFLATED;
    public static final int NO_COMPRESSION;
    public static final int BEST_SPEED;
    public static final int BEST_COMPRESSION;
    public static final int DEFAULT_COMPRESSION;
    public static final int FILTERED;
    public static final int HUFFMAN_ONLY;
    public static final int DEFAULT_STRATEGY;
    public synchronized native void setDictionary(byte[] buf,
        int off, int len);
    public synchronized native int deflate(byte[] buf, int off,
        int len);
    public synchronized native int getTotalIn();
    public synchronized native int getTotalOut();
    public synchronized native void reset();
    public synchronized native void end();
    public Deflater(int level, boolean nowrap)
    public Deflater(int level)
    public Deflater()
    protected void finalize()
    public synchronized void finish()
    public synchronized boolean finished()
    public boolean needsInput()
    public synchronized void setInput(byte[] buf, int off, int
        len)
    public synchronized void setLevel(int Level)
    public synchronized void setStrategy(int strategy)
    static
```

java.util.zip.DeflaterOutputStream

This resembles Deflater (see "java.util.zip.Deflater" in this part for details), but it sends the output to a stream instead of to a byte array.

```
public class DeflaterOutputStream extends FilterOutputStream
    protected Deflater def;
    protected byte[] buf;
    public void close() throws IOException
    protected void deflate() throws IOException
    public DeflaterOutputStream(OutputStream out, Deflater def,
        int size)
    public DeflaterOutputStream(OutputStream out, Deflater def)
    public void write(int b) throws IOException
    public void write(byte[] buf, int off, int len) throws
        IOException
```

java.util.zip.GZIPInputStream

GZIPInputStream reads compressed data from a stream. The class accepts data in the GZIP format.

```
public class GZIPInputStream extends InflaterInputStream
    protected CRC32 crc;
    protected boolean eos;
    public final static int GZIP_MAGIC;
    public synchronized void close() throws IOException
    public GZIPInputStream(InputStream in, int size) throws
        IOException
    public GZIPInputStream(InputStream in) throws IOException
    public synchronized int read(byte[] buf, int off, int len)
        throws IOException
```

java.util.zip.GZIPOutputStream

This class writes compressed data to a stream using the GZIP format.

```
public class GZIPOutputStream extends DeflaterOutputStream
    protected CRC32 crc;
    public synchronized void close() throws IOException
    public GZIPOutputStream(OutputStream out, int size) throws
        IOException
    public GZIPOutputStream(OutputStream out) throws IOException
    public synchronized void write(byte[] buf, int off, int len)
        throws IOException
```

java.util.zip.Inflater

Inflater performs compression using the ZLIB compression library. Inflater takes a byte array and produces a compressed byte array. See "java.util.zip.Deflater" in this part for methods to decompress a byte array using the ZLIB library.

```
public class Inflater
    public synchronized native void setDictionary(byte[] buf,
        int off, int len);
    public synchronized native int inflate(byte[] buf, int off,
        int len) throws DataFormatException;
    public synchronized native int getAdler();
    public synchronized native int getTotalIn();
    public synchronized native int getTotalOut();
    public synchronized native void reset();
    public synchronized native void end();
    protected void finalize()
    public synchronized boolean finished()
    public synchronized int getRemaining()
    public Inflater(boolean nowrap)
    public Inflater()
    public synchronized boolean needsDictionary()
    public synchronized boolean needsInput()
    public synchronized void setInput(byte[] buf, int off, int
        len)
```

java.util.zip.InflaterInputStream

InflaterInputStream resembles Inflater (see "java.util. zip.Inflater" in this part for more information), but it takes the input from a stream instead of a byte array.

```
public class InflaterInputStream extends FilterInputStream
    protected Inflater inf;
    protected byte[] buf;
    protected int len;
    protected void fill() throws IOException
    public InflaterInputStream(InputStream in, Inflater inf, int
        size)
    public InflaterInputStream(InputStream in, Inflater inf)
    public int read() throws IOException
    public int read(byte[] buf, int off, int len) throws
        IOException
    public long skip(long n) throws IOException
```

java.util.zip.ZipConstants

ZipConstants contains some constants used by the ZLIB compression classes.

```
interface ZipConstants
    static long LOCSIG;
    static long EXTSIG;
    static long CENSIG;
    static long ENDSIG;
    static final int LOCHDR;
    static final int EXTHDR;
    static final int CENHDR;
    static final int ENDHDR;
    static final int LOCVER;
    static final int LOCFLG;
    static final int LOCHOW;
    static final int LOCTIM;
    static final int LOCCRC;
    static final int LOCSIZ;
    static final int LOCLEN;
    static final int LOCNAM;
    static final int LOCEXT;
    static final int EXTCRC;
    static final int EXTSIZ;
    static final int EXTLEN;
    static final int CENVEM;
    static final int CENVER;
    static final int CENFLG;
    static final int CENHOW;
    static final int CENTIM;
    static final int CENCRC;
    static final int CENSIZ;
    static final int CENLEN;
    static final int CENNAM;
    static final int CENEXT;
    static final int CENCOM;
    static final int CENDSK;
    static final int CENATT;
    static final int CENATX;
    static final int CENOFF;
```

```
static final int ENDSUB;
static final int ENDTOT;
static final int ENDSIZ;
static final int ENDOFF;
static final int ENDCOM;
```

java.util.zip.ZipEntry

This class represents an entry in a ZIP file. The ZipFile class uses ZipEntry.

```
public class ZipEntry implements ZipConstants
    String name;
    long time;
    long size;
    long offset;
    byte[] extra;
    String comment;
    int flag;
    int method;
    int version;
    long crc;
    long csize;
    public String getComment()
    public long getCompressedSize()
    public long getCrc()
    public byte[] getExtra()
    public String getName()
    public long getSize()
    public long getTime()
    public boolean isDirectory()
    public void setComment(String comment)
    public void setCrc(long crc)
    public void setExtra(byte[] extra)
    public void setName(String name)
    public void setSize(long size)
    public void setTime(long time)
    public String toString()
    public String toString(boolean detailed)
    public ZipEntry(String name)
    public ZipEntry()
```

java.util.zip.ZipFile

ZipFile represents a zip file. Use the getEntry() method to retrieve a single zip entry.

```
public class ZipFile implements ZipConstants
    RandomAccessFile raf;
    long cenpos;
    long pos;
    public void close() throws IOException
    public Enumeration entries()
    public ZipEntry getEntry(String name)
    public InputStream getInputStream(ZipEntry e) throws
        ZipException, IOException
    public String getName()
    static final long getUInt(byte b[], int off)
```

(continued)

(continued)
```
static final int getUShort(byte b[], int off)
synchronized int read(long pos, byte b[], int off, int len)
   throws IOException
synchronized int read(long pos) throws IOException
static final void setBytes(byte b[], int off, int len, int
   v)
public ZipFile(String name) throws ZipException, IOException
public ZipFile(File file) throws ZipException, IOException
```

java.util.zip.ZipInputStream

ZipInputStream reads data from a stream in ZIP format.
ZipInputStream differs from ZipFile because it accepts data
from an arbitrary InputStream.

```
public class ZipInputStream extends InflaterInputStream
implements ZipConstants
    public synchronized void closeEntry() throws ZipException,
       IOException
    public synchronized ZipEntry getNextEntry() throws
       ZipException, IOException
    public synchronized int read(byte[] buf, int off, int len)
       throws ZipException, IOException
    public long skip(long n) throws ZipException, IOException
    public ZipInputStream(InputStream in)
```

java.util.zip.ZipOutputStream

ZipOutputStream writes data to a stream in ZIP format.
ZipOutputStream is similar to the ZipFile class; the main
difference is that this class can write data to an arbitrary
OutputStream.

```
public class ZipOutputStream extends DeflaterOutputStream
implements ZipConstants
    public static final int STORED;
    public static final int DEFLATED;
    public synchronized void close() throws ZipException,
       IOException
    public synchronized void closeEntry() throws ZipException,
       IOException
    public synchronized void putNextEntry(ZipEntry e) throws
       ZipException, IOException
    public void setComment(String comment)
    public void setLevel(int level)
    public void setMethod(int method)
    public synchronized void write(byte[] buf, int off, int len)
       throws ZipException, IOException
    public ZipOutputStream(OutputStream out)
```

Java Errors and Exceptions

Part IV uses hierarchy diagrams to show you all the errors and exceptions associated with the packages discussed in this book. The classes we list in this part are all subclasses of `java.lang.Error` or `java.lang.Exception`, but these subclasses are part of several different packages, as well.

We know you will find the class hierarchy diagrams very useful tools. The Java compiler forces you to catch all exceptions that are not a subclass of `RunTimeException` or `Error`. From the diagrams, you can easily identify which exceptions must be caught. You may want to catch some of the exceptions subclasses from `RunTimeException` as well, because these errors and exceptions will be fatal if not caught.

Remember: All exceptions and errors are subclassed from `java.lang.Throwable`. Refer to that class in Part III for additional methods, such as `getMessage()`.

In this part . . .

✔ **Making exceptions**

✔ **Uncovering errors**

Looking at Java Exceptions

TIP

The following diagram shows you some common exceptions that occur in Java. All the classes in this diagram are subclasses of java.lang.Exception, but they show exception classes that are common to all packages.

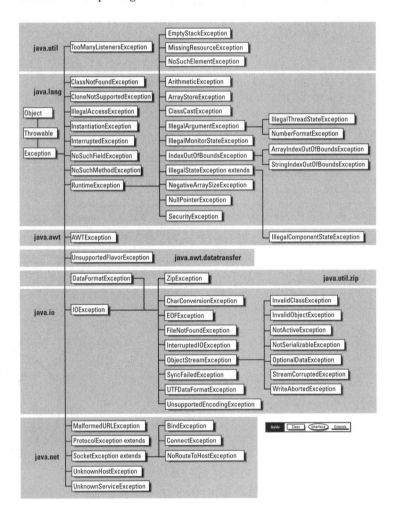

Picking out Java Errors

The following diagram shows you some common errors that occur in Java. All the classes in this diagram are subclasses of `java.lang.Error`, but they show error classes that are common to all packages.

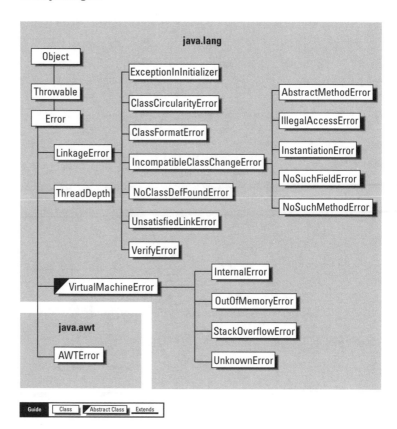

Index

RETURN THIS
REGISTRATION CARD
FOR FREE CATALOG

Title of this book: **Java™ API For Dummies® QR**

My overall rating of this book:
❑ Very good [1]   ❑ Good [2]   ❑ Satisfactory [3]   ❑ Fair [4]   ❑ Poor [5]

IDG BOOKS

THE WORLD OF
COMPUTER
KNOWLEDGE

How I first heard about this book:
❑ Found in bookstore; name: [6]
❑ Book review: [7]
❑ Advertisement: [8]
❑ Catalog: [9]
❑ Word of mouth; heard about book from friend, co-worker, etc.: [10]
❑ Other: [11]

What I liked most about this book:

What I would change, add, delete, etc., in future editions of this book:

Other comments:

Number of computer books I purchase in a year: ❑ 1 [12] ❑ 2-5 [13] ❑ 6-10 [14] ❑ More than 10 [15]

I would characterize my computer skills as:
❑ Beginner [16]   ❑ Intermediate [17]   ❑ Advanced [18]   ❑ Professional [19]
I use ❑ DOS [20]   ❑ Windows [21]   ❑ OS/2 [22]   ❑ Unix [23]   ❑ Macintosh [24]   ❑ Other: [25]____
(please specify)

I would be interested in new books on the following subjects:
(please check all that apply, and use the spaces provided to identify specific software)

❑ Word processing: [26]   ❑ Spreadsheets: [27]
❑ Data bases: [28]   ❑ Desktop publishing: [29]
❑ File Utilities: [30]   ❑ Money management: [31]
❑ Networking: [32]   ❑ Programming languages: [33]
❑ Other: [34]

I use a PC at (please check all that apply): ❑ home [35] ❑ work [36] ❑ school [37] ❑ other: [38] _____
The disks I prefer to use are ❑ 5.25 [39]   ❑ 3.5 [40]   ❑ other: [41]_____

I have a CD ROM: ❑ yes [42]   ❑ no [43]

I plan to buy or upgrade computer hardware this year: ❑ yes [44]   ❑ no [45]

I plan to buy or upgrade computer software this year: ❑ yes [46]   ❑ no [47]

Name: _____ Business title: [48]
Type of Business: [49]
Address (❑ home [50] ❑ work [51]/Company name: _____)
Street/Suite#
City [52]/State [53]/Zipcode [54]: _____ Country [55]

❑ **I liked this book!**
You may quote me by name in future IDG Books Worldwide promotional materials.

My daytime phone number is _____

❏ YES!

Please keep me informed about IDG's World of Computer Knowledge. Send me the latest IDG Books catalog.